Advance Praise for *Daydreams*

"Wow! If you've ever questioned why God allowed personal pain or tragic circumstances to enter your life or the life of a loved one, this book is for you! Writing as a modern day 'Job', Daniel communicates with brutal and graphic honesty of his (literally) gut wrenching journey with physical, mental, emotional and spiritual pain on his pathway to learning what it really means to 'trust in the Lord.' I highly recommend this book."

Dennis J Keating
Senior Pastor, Emmanuel Faith Community Church

"In this very personal story, Dan takes the reader through a physical war zone that at times is unbelievable but totally true. As you identify with his struggles, you will see the bright light of God's power shinning through every disappointment and every victory.
Dan's faith in God to take him through every physical twist and turn in his life can only instill in the reader the confidence to know that God is always in charge and that He loves us with incredible love."

Jim Smoke: Author, Speaker and Life Coach

"*Daydreams* is a gripping reality check for our lives—our dreams, the pain we experience and our view of God. Daniel Parkins writes with a compelling vulnerability that will immediately draw you in. His fascinating and tragic story, woven together with rock solid biblical truth makes Daydreams a powerful and important book."

Jeramy Clark,
Author of *I Gave Dating A Chance, He's HOT She's HOT, Define The Relationship, After You Drop Them Off*

DAYDREAMS

daydreams
An End to My Nightmares

DANIEL PARKINS

TATE PUBLISHING & *Enterprises*

To Kelly

You are my constant; my dream; my ambition.
You loved me in my pain,
Kissed me in my doubts,
and held me during my nightmares.
You are always and forever beautiful to me.
I love this chance to grow old with you.

acknowledgements

thanking God, I feel an overwhelming sense of gratitude to so many people in my life. The support I have felt has been tremendous and to mention all of those I am thankful for would be impossibly long. However, during the process of writing this book, one person more than all made it possible for others to read and process so that the Lord could use these words to minister to those who are broken, hurting, or confused. That woman, by the grace of God, took up the call to edit my shabby collection of words and turned it into what it is today. It is to her that I proclaim the main source of thankfulness as she unselfishly spent many hours and nights away from her amazing family to see this project completed. Though she wasn't there to experience the trials in my life, she was there to make sense of it all. Thank you Mary Petrie, and thank you Father for putting her in my life to help with this endeavor.

There were many times when I wrote these words that I found myself in Mammoth Lakes, California, in a house not my own. The love expressed to me from one man humbles me still today, as he loved me unconditionally. Ed Bellamy has become a hero of mine, and through his dedication and thoughtfulness to me during a very tumultuous time in my life, I want to express my dire love and thankfulness to him as well. He is a pillar of strength to me and a light during the fog of war that I had to wade through. Also, more than a light to me, and someone more dear and loved than most, is my Meme, and I want to thank her for being immovable to me. She showed me the power of God through looking to Him despite our present circumstances and has taught me so much. I love you and your Kleenex.

While I dedicate this book to my wife Kelly, there is no part of me that was able to move forward in the future without the love and support of my angel, Kim Bellamy, brothers Josh and Todd and my father Barry Parkins. My wife's family, (among them the entire Hoffmann house including Peter, Janie, Laura, and Kathleen), as well as the Carabba crew (Shauna, Nick, Kaeden, Nathan, Shaye and the new addition of Naomi), took me in and loved me as a son and brother. I couldn't have asked for a better family to marry into as they showed their unconditional love for me despite my failures. One time in particular, when awaiting my second liver transplant, they came and visited me in the hospital, bringing more love than I could ever express. This love defines them.

Finally, as his mother was instrumental in the formation of Daydreams, I want to thank Joshua Petrie for all of his work in the DVD-ROM that was produced before publication. I was blessed to speak in different countries and places in the U.S., and Josh, through his hard work, brilliant design and intense dedication, made a beautiful layout for my words to be read by many. You are my *big* little brother, and I miss you.

contents

introduction

many dreams I have had; many dreams that have haunted me, encouraged me, strengthened me and frightened me in the waking hours of the night. When the darkness rolls over my bed like a daunting figure eager to take my breath away, and the sickly pale moonlight finds shelter between the folds of my comforter, nightmares and dreams have overtaken me. In those dreams, thousands of stories have been told in the recesses of my mind, thousands of battles fought and no doubt won, thousands of loves lost and loves gained. No matter what happens in those dreams, I am able to wake up from their pseudo-reality, finding true comfort in the absolute goodness of life and breath. No matter the amount of pain experienced or the crippling fear that was conjured up, I could always awaken with the refreshing noise of the sun breaking through my pitted windows and the chorus of birds singing their praises to the Lord. What a pleasant thing indeed!

It was that reality actualized, the one in which I move and breathe, where we all dwell yesterday, today, and tomorrow. When we dream, do our bills get paid? Does our schooling get completed? Are our errands accomplished? If we were content to "live" in these dreams, nothing tangible, nothing good, nothing of substance would ever come to fruition.

Just as our bodies fall asleep on our comfortable pillows each night and long for that blissful state of rest and dreamland, so our minds are walking around every day in a state of dreams, sleeping against the realities that are right in front of us. And those realities are never more hidden than when we are facing trials in our lives. Pain fogs the mind, trials and heartache make the soul lose its grip on reality, and in the midst of that pain, we are a people who long for daydream realities where we are the masters of our minds.

Most of us have had dreams where we wake up and swear that it actually happened. The deep sleeps where fiction met reality, where you could feel the love, taste the foods, wince from the pain; where you could remember with vivid clarity the tiny cottage among the hills and vineyards just outside of Rome, half expecting to see the structure in some tourism package where you visited the night before. When the sun shone so brightly in the morning's hue, you half expected to wake up with a sunburn. As if you could wake up and expect your wife or husband, friend or relative to reminisce with you over coffee or tea and a good laugh about some Italian chef everyone affectionately called "Papa Joe" who was actually a woman. Dreams that were so close to reality, it almost seemed unfair that they weren't, as if you were robbed of a precious gift you received the night before.

But most of our dreams are dictated from our experiences of what is real, the sights and sounds throughout our actual waking existence. Our view of trials is much the same; we have a tiny grasp of the truth, yet plagiarize, romanticize, and morph the truth into what we desire it to be. I believe that we live in false realities today when it comes to trials, living in a dream world. Some dwell in the midst of a nightmare, as you will see my life thus far has mirrored, but nonetheless, we need to wake up and experience the freedom of God's perfection in sovereignty.

There are dreams in my story that are meant to show the trains of thought I had in the midst of my struggles; trains of thought such as naïveté, control, the feelings of being alone, anger, and many more. Some of them actually happened; some of them were actual dreams. But in all of them, I woke up from their "reality."

I invite you, the reader, on a journey with me through my life, soul, and mind. These stories are me, over an eight-year period that was one walking nightmare, until I realized the goodness of the Lord outside of it all, the freedom of trusting in a God that is so much more than me. My prayer is that you will find some comfort between these pages, some things to relate to, some things that you find horrific. In no way do I claim to have the strength that has gotten me through these trials, the strength that has brought me through to having a blessed trust in my Savior. The source of that strength came only from the Lord, and it is to Him that all the glory belongs.

naiveté

i never thought that I would see my best friend die right before my very eyes; then again, I never thought I would see death, apart from having the television as my shield to that reality. That kind of stuff was only make-believe, right? You know, the stuff in movies where we lose ourselves in fantasy and escape reality, where Yoda gives advice and William Wallace yells "Freedom"; the kind of fantasy where you cheer in the theaters when the villain dies, and only the most grotesque of deaths will do; when sick days were spent watching the Goonies over and over again, and feeling "the Force" was as easy as making your bed?

I lost that naïveté at the age of fourteen, when my grandfather, my "Pop," my best friend, had an aneurysm on the golf course right before me. That fateful morning, the one that stole my innocence, began with breakfast at Pop's favorite restaurant right on the bay near San Luis Obispo. He had eggs and bacon, and put more salt and pepper on them than any two people would, and after we finished, we donned our golf garb and headed to my favorite tournament of the year.

There was an electricity on the newly cut grass that morning. Expectations ran far ahead of reality, and amidst the hundred plus member field, I searched the cosmos for the strength to make it past the nerves that ripped me apart. When your adrenaline pumps, you inevitably rush to the bathroom to release the wastes that your kidneys have just filtered, and I remember doing so a number of times before my tee-off.

The Avila Bay Member-Guest Golf Tournament was the biggest of the year, and we were knee-deep in the middle of it. It was the second day and we were leading the field by a narrow margin, which wasn't too bad considering we had a two-man team consisting of a fourteen year old who had an eight handicap, and a sixty-nine year old who had a twenty-two handicap.

The entire morning was spent struggling to maintain our lead, yet it was also marred by intense pain in my Pop's chest. I can remember very clearly, before we headed off to hit golf balls on the driving range, Pop complaining of chest pains, and my own father and I looking at each other with a sense of worry. Pop shrugged it off, but I can't help but think what would have happened had we paid more attention to his statement of pain . . .

The seventh hole, a par four dog leg left, was where Pop began to struggle. The wind was blowing slightly in our faces, and as he reached down to tee up his pure white golf ball, I heard a moan. This was the first tee box where Pop had not told a joke, and in my innocence, I sensed nothing. Swinging without taking a practice stroke, he duffed a ball off to the left into a small ravine. I hit my shot to the right of the fairway, cutting through the wind and spraying up grass as it came to a halt. He told me to take the golf cart to my ball, which I eagerly did, as he walked to find his own ball.

Thinking back on that day, I remember him being very distant when he told me to do that, and I have no doubt the pain was the source of his thoughts. I wish Pop would have said something there, there in the quiet of the morning when only the birds could be heard singing and the wind rushing past fallen leaves. I remember asking my grandmother, whom I affectionately call Meme, why Pop did not say anything, and she simply said, "Daniel, because playing golf with you was his favorite thing to do, and nothing could take him away from that joy." I guess the same stubborn blood runs through my veins.

I can remember holding a four iron with little over 170 yards to the pin when I noticed Pop searching around for his golf ball ahead of me. You see, he missed his second shot as well and was looking for it right in my line of sight to the pin. I looked at my ball to picture what approach I was going to take, all the while having memories of "Golf Vision" running through my head.

When his body fell, my make-believe reality came to a standstill, and all I could do was look forward at his body on the ground. I had never seen his body lying on the ground before, and I knew that this was the beginning of an awful reality.

I yelled at him to get up. I noticed the face that I had looked to for security and hope, laughter and warmth was now down on the ground. It was the face that donned the brightest smile whenever I needed it most, and the face that wrinkled with affection as he held me in my nightmares. I don't really remember what I was thinking at that moment, but rest assured that my young mind was not prepared for what happened.

Silence came. In a matter of seconds, my innocence was ripped from me, and my naïveté shattered as I ran to him. Running was like a dream in which everything paused. The wind stopped, and the leaves seemed to float in mid-air.

Ten feet away I stopped, and I started to scream at the top of my lungs. I looked behind me and found my father waiting on the tee box behind us, for it was his foursome that was trailing us. I ran as fast as I could and couldn't utter anything from my mouth except the words, "Dad! Dad! Dad!" My heart pounded as increased shots of adrenaline surged through my veins. Each step I took stripped away a percentage of my hope as I came closer to my now pale best friend. The look on my father's face was horror, as he knew exactly what had happened the moment I screamed. Without a moment's hesitation he flew to his cart, stepped on the pedal and took off to meet my frantic cry.

"Pop's on the ground, Dad, Pop's on the ground!" Tears found a home on my cheeks that afternoon.

My father's cart didn't even stop near me but raced to where Pop's body was and stopped a few feet away. He jumped out, turned him over, and immediately checked his pulse. As my dad's hands fumbled to find it, I hoped against hope that there was some sign of life.

Though it was a warm day in the summer, I remember having that chill right before one vomits. Time stood still again as the reality of death broke down my walls with a sledge hammer. I was alone, though there were many people around me. As I looked at Pop's face with fear, I tried to find comfort in wishing for a dream. His face will be forever etched into my memory, and the scenes that followed have haunted me many a night in the cold depths of my mind. To this day, there are times when his picture grabs me and sends me to that place, that fairway that stole something from me.

CPR was performed on Pop as soon as my Dad couldn't find a pulse, and the blood that flowed from his mouth to the ground shocked me.

I found out later that shrapnel during a World War II battle in the Pacific Theater from a grenade had exploded near Pop. The surgeons at the time couldn't remove all of the shrapnel from his heart. Years later, that same shrapnel inched its way into his heart valves, finally impeding enough blood flow to produce an explosion in his heart. The doctors say that there wasn't much pain, that it was one brief moment of torment but nothing lasting. Who knows really? But I do know that he was feeling something that morning and didn't say anything, and it wasn't for some brief period.

Five to ten minutes later the ambulance arrived and took over for my dad, who was performing CPR. By that time, Pop's body was severely bloated from having air blown into him and not having any released. His eyes were cold and lifeless, and his skin color was non-existent. Blood was all over his face; and on my dad's face, I could see the frustration mixed with Pop's blood. Over my dad's shoulder, I looked down on him and saw something that wasn't Pop, some-thing different. Pop was reduced to a form unlike any I had ever seen. No amount of sick TV shows or the numbing reality of the nature channel could prepare me for such an attack on my senses. It was as if I was seeing the reality of life for the first time in the death of my grandfather, my Pop. His body was lifeless and dead, and at that moment, rage and fury flooded my senses.

I ran and didn't care where I was running to. Feeling the freshly watered grass beneath my feet and screaming to God, I cursed Him with all the words that a naïve fourteen-year-old could muster in his mind and didn't stop crying for quite some time.

If I could only tell Pop one more time that I loved him, if I could only be hugged by him in his old arms one more time, if I could only see him smile, then I would be happy. I hate clichés, but this one is true: "You never know what you have until it is gone." And Pop was gone.

Everything happened quickly once Pop was put into the ambulance and I was jetted away to the hospital to await the verdict on Pop's life. I remember riding in the passenger seat as my dad and I spoke without words. Worry was what filled my heart along with a sense of dread for the inevitability of what lay ahead. Just sitting there helpless while Dad drove was tough; I felt like the leather seats were burning a hole in my pants because I wanted to run quicker than the car was going. I remember that we got off at an exit called Oso Avenue; that street name will be etched in my mind forever.

Sitting there in the car, with nothing to do but pray to a God I was unfamiliar with, I dreamed:

DAYDREAM

The sun was behind the clouds that day, hiding its penetrating glare amidst the settling mist that formed like a blanket over the pocket of Mendocino. We were both running to catch up with his John Deere tractor that slowly cut the emerald grass beneath our tiny feet. I laughed as I tripped and my cousin came running to me. I tripped her as I was on the ground and made her tumble down to me, and we both laughed uncontrollably. *Pop yelled from behind his back that he was going to mow us with the lawn if we weren't careful. So we jetted off into the long grass that was almost as tall as us and was seen as the boundary of Pop's property.*

Disappearing quickly into the underbrush, we became the hunters of Kilimanjaro, on a Safari to catch the rare and mysterious beasts that ravaged the countryside and pillaged the nearby towns with reckless abandon. As we crept low to the ground with the thunderous blade cutter reverberating beyond our horizon, we looked for bent grass and any sign of fresh tracks to pursue.

My faithful companion, Hope, stumbled across some fresh tracks, and with a hunched back and cat-like reflexes, stepped over a log and tripped on her face. With moments and seconds as precious as a first love, I raced over to her as fast as a bullet from a deadly gun. Getting her to her feet was no easy task with the help from my underdeveloped muscles. As every sinew ripped from my body, the team of hunters was off again. We ran through the grass as if it was going out of style, like our last chance to wear platforms at a disco in the eighties. And after we stopped running, we ran some more. We were at that age when you could run and not grow tired. As C.S. Lewis writes at the end of The Last Battle, *all the creatures ran. Imagine, being able to run and not grow tired. Who would ever stop? Who would end the exuberant feeling of the wind against your face? Like the puppy sticking its head out of a fast moving car. Freedom. Freedom of knowing that everything is as it should be. Freedom.*

Our path winded left and right, left and right, further into the unknown. We stopped, for what fell into our eyes was the beast we were hunting. Slithering this way and that, we saw the green scales blend into the grass as a gopher burrows into the ground. Quickly now, or it might escape.

Up ahead of us lay a small pond with creatures inhabiting their self-made village, continuing on into infinity without the aid of man or science. So much life, so much potential, and all we could do was pursue our frightened prey. It was the food that we needed to survive, the nectar that made our juices flow. Reaching down, I touched its tail, and it squirmed between my fingers, hissing all the while. Beautiful. "Hope, quick, gather the rest of the hunters, we can't let this one get away!"

Without a moment's hesitation, she attempted to jump on the beast, which had a habit of sticking out its tongue to feel for its next move. Barely missing the creature, we laughed and pursued it all the more. Lunging for it seemed proper, and I grabbed it between my fingers.

This snake was not the poisonous kind, for our mature intellect told us so, but I took hold of the head just in case. Surveying my accomplishment, gazing around at my surroundings, I saw a wonderfully lush life: Trees ripe with dew, bordering a calm pond that was stabbed with dead branches and leaves; swarms of insects buzzing about with their own plans and purposes; peaceful leaves; toads enjoying the calm rustle of the wind; and millions of tiny ants gathering for the coming winter.

Losing my tranquility with the sudden feeling of the serpent shimmying its way up my arm, my attention was taken back to the present situation. What to do now? Shall we vanquish our enemy, or show kindness to something that has no idea of right or wrong, only the strong instinct of survival?

"Can I hold it, Danny?"

My cousin Hope lashed out in an effort to grab hold of that which we had pursued and used so much energy to obtain.

Fumbling, falling. Our struggle between who would hold it ended in confusion, and our prisoner found a way to evade us. We both landed on the ground, holding nothing but dirt.

Reaching the safety of the long grass, the snake slithered frantically away, never to be found again. A feeling of loss and anger flooded my senses and passed as quickly as found.

"Hope, Danny, breakfast is ready!"

A surreal reality invaded our senses: no longer the hunters of the pasture, but the ravaging animals ourselves. Racing to see who could get to the house first became the only thought in our minds. I lost a snake that day, but I had love to go back to. A love that was always there, pouring itself out into our every pore, a love that would never fade.

As the car made a series of lefts and rights to where the hospital signs were pointing, memories of Pop flooded my mind. Memories of laughter and times of warmth near his wonderful fireplace. My grandparents' cabin in Mendocino was where I loved to go and where my dreams would often take me whenever I laid my head to rest. Memories of going on Pop's fishing boat, which was no bigger than a large car but took us beyond the great unknown of the sea, and memories of Pop telling stories as the raccoons would chew holes in his deck raced through my mind. Making boats out of 2x4s and balsa wood that we would send down the creeks of Mendocino near their home was my favorite. Though they would inevitably sink, Pop was always there with another idea on how to improve them.

Those memories plague me with a sense of grief, coupled with a joy that I do at least have them, but I feel as though I was robbed because of the short time I was able to spend with a man I respect more than most. I only wish he could have been there when I graduated high school and that he would be there when I get married and when I have my first child.

The one thing that I remember, from all of what happened to me that fateful morning in August, is the way I last saw Pop. Not when he was alive, but the last time I saw him in this world. We were in the hospital and he was just pronounced dead, though he died there out on the golf course, and I saw something that I will never forget. I saw a white sheet covering his lifeless body that was extended over his head. My dad had me peek in the room because he wanted me to remember something that I always will. He said, "Danny, I want you to remember this, for not too many men will see this. You see your Pop right there, well, what is he wearing on his feet?"

And that was what made the pain of losing Pop not so bad. Many men have died doing things that they have to do, or being sick in a hospital bed. But not my Pop, he had died with his golf cleats on. He had died playing in a golf tournament with his grandson. He had died doing his favorite thing.

I still miss Pop, and think of him often.

As I said earlier, his face still haunts my dreams from time to time, and whenever I visit my wonderful Meme, my thoughts inevitably drift to him. Pictures of Pop are still prominently displayed around her house and his "spirit" still dwells upon her lips. I remember driving her home one weekend after visiting my mother in Mammoth Lakes, pulling into the garage and fighting against a passion to release the floodgates of tears I had hidden for Pop for so long. Meme's mate, her lifetime companion, was gone, and she was left lonely at night.

She had moved out to Palm Desert in hopes of living out the rest of her life in the company of my mother, who had promised to live out there with my father before the divorce was on his lips. She, too, had become a casualty of that sin, and more than anyone else, she had been affected.

Now, when I see her, I see an older woman who has the spirit of an angel and a woman who has had her walls crushed one after the other.

Meme is strong, and insists on not becoming the victim. She has taught me an invaluable lesson, one that will ring true in my ears for the rest of my days. As I stood in her kitchen the afternoon I dropped her off from the visit with my mother, I stood staring at a mirror with tears in my eyes. This was only weeks ago, so it is still very fresh in my mind.

With the salt from tears stinging my eyes, I asked selfishly how she does it. How does she get out of bed every morning, clean the already spotless house, and go about her day knowing that most of her life is spent alone?

With the familiar scent of grandma's house wafting to my senses, she told me resolutely that life is about our mental approach. She said that it's about a decision that one makes every single day. She said very simply that you can concentrate on the bad things in life, or you can concentrate on the good things in life. Each day she gets out of bed, making a decision to concentrate on the good things she has, all the things with which she is blessed.

I would venture to say that Meme is happier than most in this world, and that she has more joy than those who have far more possessions. She is an inspiration to me and always will be. I love my Meme.

LEARNING

I wonder how many people actually play the victim from day to day, barely getting by. Do you? Do you see your life as a set of tragedies, one after the other, trying to make sense of a God who is suppose to be all loving? Each Sunday, I preach to many college-aged young adults, and I look out among them only to see a certain helplessness.

"Blessed are the poor in spirit, for theirs is the Kingdom of Heaven." (Matthew 5.3) How can this truth make us understand anything about our individual plights? Does that help someone deal with the death of a lifelong companion? How cruel is it for Jesus to proclaim these words to this generation, a generation so influenced by the circumstances we see around us? To be poor in spirit is to recognize one's spiritual poor-ness apart from this loving God who came down to die for us. It is to realize how we actually are.

Yet, do these words offer any comfort? Of course they do not, for we are a generation in search of tangible things, those little things that make us feel better about ourselves. We need comfort in the form of something we can touch, not something we hear. Faith is ousted and the philosophy of touch is hailed as king. We no longer care about truth in the face of pain and suffering, but we desire the remedy to help us forget, to help us move on. The things that salve our miseries are the gifts of God, yet we don't see the God behind those gifts. Most of the time, we don't even care who is the source of that specific gift; we only care about the ointment itself.

During the death of my Pop, I had a close family, one that was there for me unlike any other and really became a cornerstone of healing for me. I was able to talk about my problems, talk about my worries, and talk about the anger that quickly welled up inside of me. Yet at that time, could the offer of being "poor in spirit" do anything for my little naïve psyche?

No, but even at that young age, I realized that I didn't have all of the answers, that it was okay to doubt, as the psalmists do time and time again, yet I was able to come back to what I needed most . . . my Savior. I realized that I needed Him most, because I knew that I didn't have the answers myself, only the emotions that asked the questions.

We would do well, and this is no easy task, to realize our plight. Yet here I go, standing on my soapbox, offering a salve that is laced with salt to some. What good is it to be poor in spirit? Is it not better to be rich in spirit? Surely this is the case, at least it's the philosophy that muddles our minds currently. Heck, we are the masters of our own destinies, relying on ourselves as the moderns we have come to be. Man has the answers and needs no one to come to. To go to God is seen as a weakness, yet all do in times of dire need. All go to God in times of great fear that humbles us to our cores. All go to God with great questions that no one can answer. We yell at the God we so fervently try to deny in our actions, taunting Him to answer a people who do not love Him, for only He knows. Yet do we deserve an answer? Does Meme deserve an answer for the death of the love of her life? Most would take up the call, raise the banner and yell, "absolutely!" We try to find answers, yet we know we will not get them.

There are those that have no sense of the God who created them, and when they get no answer from their half-hearted petitions, they become only more confirmed in their minds and in their dogmatic beliefs that there is actually no God. Yet again, when the next major hurdle in their lives springs forth like a terrible plague, on whom do they thrust their questions?

And again, when God seemingly doesn't answer the way they want Him to, in their own infinite wisdom and perfect plan, they grow embittered towards a God that they say "doesn't exist." Such is the sad spiral of termination that runs through the blood of our thinking.

I think Meme, more than most, deserved an explanation; yet, in her poor-ness of spirit, she rested in the arms of a God that took care of her every need. Was she physically touched in some way? No doubt, by the loved ones around her, yet not by the God who spurred on those to love her in the first place. But she found joy in the gifts from her Creator. She also knew her limitations and knew, as Mother Teresa succinctly noted, that "*the worst life on earth is but one night in a dirty hotel room compared to eternity.*"

I realize that this is all great to hear, but it really does nothing in the form of comforting the broken. But you know just as much as I that God does not leave us broken but instead heals us beautifully. I didn't just sit there on the hospital floor weeping my eyes into oblivion; I was able to see the wonderful love of God through that last image of Pop.

Those who come to the Lord with broken hearts do not leave with broken hearts also. Relying on Him will not disappoint. But relying on a God who may not always touch us physically is a hard thing to do with the world screaming in our ears to think otherwise.

If we can somehow see the world, see how our minds have so been influenced by the desire to kill the God that actually gives us freedom from pain and suffering, then we can begin to let the Lord heal us of deep wounds. In giving up the philosophy that says we should have a life filled with joy and nothing else—to be happy is to be rich, fame is all that matters—in giving up the influence that has permeated our souls, we will "inherit" the philosophy of God. No one has the answers to pain or disease or death, but God showers the love behind the answers that lead us to such things.

Much behind this way of thinking is our lack of belief in a Holy God. God is holy, or so we read from His Word, yet we have no concept of the Holy One. It is imperative to understand where this lack of holiness comes from.

Ours is a generation filled with itself, needing to grasp something to attain some semblance of control, and when unable to grasp the heart of holiness, we base our beliefs off of other avenues or trains of thought around us.

When we view holiness, we have an underlying knowledge of something else, for in order to truly grasp something, it must be compared to something familiar, something we can hold on to. That something that we can hold on to that leads us to an idea of holiness is respect, stemmed from our interactions with those who have "earned it." But it was not always like this. At one time—and please bear with me as I believe this is pertinent to the issue of trials—mankind believed in a geo-centric universe, one that revolved around the earth. The earth was at one time believed to be the center of the universe. Because of certain discoveries, however, we came to see the sun in all its glory and life-giving heat as the center of our universe. Currently, in this post-modern age that seeks significance above all, we have crossed the realm of the sun being the center of the universe, a helio-centric way of thinking, to a homo-centric way of thinking that places man in the center of the cosmos.

Thus we view God as our own chauffeur or bellhop or Santa Claus or private miracle worker. And when trials come, we place God in a box and throw our expectations on Him. We are like disgruntled employers who "fire" God, looking for other "employees" to fill the spot, however tiny it was to begin with, that would satisfy and help us to feel comfortable in our minds. You can see with me the obvious strain this puts on our concept of God's holiness and our stark emphasis on the material things this world conjures in front of us to distract us. When God doesn't do what we want, when our plans do not come to fruition, we throw Him away and seek to fill the void of this disgruntlement, seeking to be the centers of the universe once again. I wonder what it would be like to live in a theo-centric cosmos, a God-centered universe.

We tend to live out our own biographies as if they were the only stories that matter, and so our idea of holiness is based on respect. If God does what we want, if He helps us in our biographies to accomplish our plans for our lives, then we will respect Him and worship Him on a contingent plan. We often reduce Him to a grand Santa Clause who needs to give us what we want, and when we don't receive what we think we need, we throw tantrums like little boys and girls on Christmas morning.

When respect is understood in the growing connotation of the post-modern culture that has engulfed our generation, it can only be seen as subjective, for it must be earned precisely according to how each individual defines it. Respect is earned not from title or position, nor any longer from history or actions. The ability to give respect is up to the individual who sees himself or herself with the power to dictate and proportionate that respect. This can be seen with half the people in this country respecting the President of the United States (maybe half would be a little too high) and the other half who don't. These people ask the question, "After all, what has *he* ever done for me, what has *he* given me?"

Another example, one I think explains our view of respect, thus our beginning beliefs of holiness, is in our view towards older generations. It used to be that age demanded respect, as wisdom was seen as a virtue. With much experience and age comes volumes thick with wisdom. Those volumes of wisdom are seen in the form of wrinkled faces, warm smiles and graying hair.

This is no longer the case, however, as the post-moderns see seniority as a nuisance. They once held an honored position in the family structure. Now, it seems that structure is no longer in tact. We often see the older generations as a burden to our specific biographies. Pleasure, technology and wealth are seen as the "good" because they might help in the advancement of our goals. But anything that gets in the way becomes a stumbling block or a nuisance because it doesn't help us attain our goals quicker. This is seen as something terrible indeed. Do we not hail the senior adults as "cool" or "hip" if they separate themselves with the trend mindset or are able to take care of themselves? At that point, these seniors are no longer a nuisance to us because they are not in the way of achieving our goals. We respect them if they are not in our "way." They then play little role in our lives as we seek out varying things to fill the void we have when God is no longer in the picture. This is doubly true for those who have handicaps, the homeless, or those who cannot take care of themselves. Sad, but it seems we will respect or tolerate them if they are not in our way. They earn our respect out of compliance and the ability to help us and not hinder us in our endeavors.

Since respect must be earned, and we seem to see and get our idea of holiness from that, we therefore make God "earn" our respect. When trials come, when things happen beyond our control and God does not bless us the way we would like, and we don't like the lessons of patience that must happen, we lose our idea of holiness, for God does not "earn" our respect.

How sad, and little wonder now, that so many push away any idea of God. He has not given us what we want. We become embittered at our lack of control, and since God has not given us the things we need in our own biographies that are seen as so important, our idea of His holiness begins to crumble. To build that up again in any way, God must prove Himself worthy in our eyes by bringing our next "perfect" plans to fruition. This is sad and ridiculous, but often times proves itself to be true. Example after example can be given for this to bolster this point of view, but the two given should suffice.

And since we have no idea of holiness nor any concept of a Holy God, we grow frustrated and resentful to the God who allows these trials to take place in our lives. We struggle so much with trying to understand why, always asking the question, "Why, God, why?"

We must wake up from our naïveté and start seeing God the way scripture declares Him to be. We must see God for who He is, not what He does or what He decides to bless us with. We can't form our theologies around the effects of God and our human understanding of them; this is too reactionary. Our understanding of God's holiness would therefore always be dictated by our present circumstances.

You may have an incredibly difficult time reading that last sentence and agreeing with it. I understand, for I have asked the questions myself, but let me end this section on this. When Job, who saw more misery than any of us, asked God to give an account for why He was allowing the things in his life to happen (for he was quickly viewing himself higher than he should have, falling into the pattern of homo-centrism), God's reaction was peculiar.

After the barrage of questions were thrown in the face of the Holy One, He did not answer but asked His own questions. God does not have to give an account of His actions nor His plan, but so many of us have this idea of holiness that must be gained by things that we can understand . . . it must be earned. I challenge you to read on, and journey with me to the end as I pray we will discover some truths together about ourselves and how we look at trials and our relationships with a God who is God.

control

i t was the middle of the day, and the school bell had just rung to let us know it was time for lunch. Feeling the grass crumble beneath my feet, I walked as quickly as I could to the bathrooms. All around me, everyone was worrying about getting their lunches from their lockers or who they were going to sit next to during lunch or maybe even some of them were worrying about the stresses of the next class's test. Not me, for I was different.

A few months earlier, we were having a conversation at the dinner table—one that only a family of all boys would have—in which my brothers were talking about the size of their bowel excrements. I know, what a great conversation. My father and brothers were bragging about the size of their excrements, and I just remained quiet. My dad asked me, "Dan, what about you?"

In a meek voice, I remember saying, "What? Oh, I haven't had a solid bowel movement for over a year."

Roaring laughter ensued until my father and mother realized that I wasn't joking. Startled, my mom asked, "What do you mean you haven't had a solid bowel movement for over a year?"

"I don't know, Mom, that is just it. I have had diarrhea for over a year now."

"Why haven't you said anything to us?"

"I don't know. I guess I just thought that it wasn't a big deal."

With that, the conversation quickly turned from a jovial conversation to a serious discussion about the fact that it *was* a major deal. Within hours, my mother had already made an appointment for the following day with the colon doctor who practiced in the area, and I had time to sleep on the night's conversation.

The next day, I went to the doctor. Despite having a little bit of nervousness, the reality of having diarrhea for over a year hadn't really set in. After all, I had other things to worry about, like getting my driver's license or who I liked in school, not unimportant things like how many times I went to the bathroom a day.

So, I went in to see the doctor and I told him what was going on. With a worried expression on his face, he told me that he needed to perform a colonoscopy.

A what?

As he explained what it was, I quickly became aware of the pressing fact that I needed to leave as soon as possible. You see, a colonoscopy is a procedure where the doctor takes a camera in the form of a long bending tube inside your rectum area, blowing air as he goes through your descending, transcending, and ascending colon . . . and you are awake during the entire procedure.

As a fifteen year old, this wasn't my idea of a good time. I will spare the details on the entire procedure, but I will interject this: the pain of that procedure was very intense because of the disease I had.

The doctor diagnosed me as having Ulcerative Colitis, a disease in which the lining of the large intestine would at times be covered in ulcerations. This disease meant that I would go to the bathroom several times a day and that I wouldn't be able to break down the necessary nutrients to keep me healthy. As the ulcerations would grow in intensity, every time excrements would pass through, the lining would rip and tear, causing bleeding and sometimes excruciating pain.

I remember being in his office after the procedure was finished, thankful that I was indeed through with it, and hearing the words that I had a "disease."

Wait a minute. I wasn't some drug addict nor did I do anything to harm myself in any way. It wasn't because of something I drank or something I ate, and I wasn't some sickly kid who didn't have a clue as to what was going on. I was me, and I shouldn't have a disease, right?

Nonetheless, I found myself thinking that I was going to be different than most other people my age, and that I would have to take medication for the rest of my life. The doctor ended the conversation with the encouraging words that everything was going to be all right and that the medication should help.

So, I come back to the story of walking in the amphitheater during lunch recess. Like I said, I was rushing to the bathroom, for that was the daily routine for me. The colon disease was attacking me and the medication didn't seem to help during the "flare-ups." The pain was excruciating and tormenting, and tears started to form in my eyes. Though it was a beautiful day out and the campus was booming with homecoming preparations, I didn't care. One thought broke through the pain, and that was the hope that I could hold the excrement in my body in time to make it to the bathroom.

Explaining the pain is a difficult thing for me, since not too many people can relate, but I liken it to an animal running through my large intestine, with a spiked helmet on, rushing to get out. I apologize for being so graphic, but it was very painful.

I had made it to the middle of the amphitheater, since the bathrooms were on the other side, and felt a sense of relief as some gas passed or made some room. I knew that had given me some more time to focus on putting one foot in front of the other so as to not release my bowels on accident. I must have looked funny as I walked across that place while holding in the excrement as tight as possible, but I knew I had only around thirty more steps to make it to the bathroom.

Ten steps later, it happened. Pain so intense, so unbearable, I couldn't help it. At age sixteen, I found myself going to the bathroom in my pants.

With utter humility at the sight of everyone noticing, and in broad daylight in the middle of the area where everyone ate their lunches (hopefully I didn't make anyone lose theirs), I lowered my head and walked as fast as I could to my car. I knew that I couldn't go to the restroom since the stain would have been very visible by the time I came out. So, I lowered my backpack as far as it would go and literally made a beeline to my car.

Each step I took pained me and shot me to a reality that humbled me beyond words. *Did people notice? Were the kids going to say stuff and point as I hurried off campus?* One foot after the other was all I concentrated on. *And look, over there, that girl is looking at me funny! Does she notice? Hurry Dan, make it to the car, make it home to your safety, where all of your cares can be drowned out and you can find sanctuary in the loving arms of your mother.*

I made it home that day with tears in my eyes, and I told my mother what had happened. She was shocked and started to cry, also. I can't imagine what she, as a parent, must have felt when I broke the news to her. But that didn't make the situation difficult for me. What made it difficult was what I saw when I lowered my pants to change my clothes. I knew that I was different and that I had a disease, but what I saw mixed with the stools was my own dark blood.

With my pants lowered, I drifted off into a dream, some place where I could remember happiness, something to take me away from the shame and disgrace I felt at that moment. Daydreams were as drugs to me. They helped me escape reality. They helped me escape the torment I faced daily.

DAYDREAM

The sun was shining, as it always does in dreams where happiness is sought out like gold. In this dream, the sun, in all of its glorious rage, touched and penetrated my skin, racking each pore and filling up my sickly body with a melanin, turning my façade a darker hue.

Feeling its warmth, I lifted the shovel out of the dirt, and flung another piece of sediment over my young shoulders. The shoulders that were dressed in army garb, in hopes to hide from the enemy that was inevitably lurking around the corner.

Hurry.

That one thought pervaded my naïve mind, and I dug religiously as if that was my only care. Out of the corner of my eye, I saw the enemy dressed in his own camouflage of browns, blacks and greens giving off a stark contrast with the barn that he was hiding behind. I acted as if I hadn't seen him. Adrenaline rushed through my veins as love's hope flows in security through a hug from a father. I dove into the worm-ridden hole that was to be my shelter from the onslaught of the metals of death that would soon come flying overhead. The enemy, known by some as "Brian," hugged the ground as if he were in a love affair with it and etched his way to my newly made foxhole.

Victory was in my reach, for in my mind it was so simple. I was the commander of my army, the leader of the pack, the general who was never questioned. Everything I came up with was right, every idea or military action was done in perfection. With the honed skills of a professional leading his men to victory, my nine year old body threw the first grenade made of packed earth and rock in the direction of the enemy. With the sounds of a near miss echoing in my ears, I feel the splutter of rocks from above my man-made hole.

As dirt flung itself against my leg, I knew that it was all but over. The enemy had scored a hit as the next grenade flew overhead. With seconds to spare, I jumped out of the foxhole with a pained look on my face, wearing visibly the wound that was inflicted. Reaching down deep inside of me for the source of strength that would gain me victory, I rolled over behind the pine tree. Shards of dirt flung past my view as the tree became my shield to this new onslaught. Taking time to breathe, I gathered my senses, took control of the situation, and threw my form of death in "Brian's" direction. A direct hit!

With confidence and an air of aristocracy, I puffed up my chest *and declared victory! The battle was won, the girl was saved, and the village was spared. Only with my act of intelligence and cunning was this victory possible, only with my precise control over every detail. We called it quits and went in for some much needed lemonade . . . after surveying my foxhole, of course.*

CONTINUED DREAM

Though there was no blood visible on those old army clothes, and though the grenade wound was only make-believe, the red in my stools was real, and I couldn't dream this terrifying reality away. No matter how hard I tried, I was slowly losing control of what I called sanity. Though my daydream battle was won, the real battle was slipping between my fingers, and I was losing steam in the engine that kept me moving.

I became more of a hermit those days, not doing the activities that I would have wished for all the world to do. As friends would go out to parties, or go to the beach on church trips, I would sometimes regretfully decline. I would come up with the excuse of being too tired. Tucked away in my heart, with the puddles of tears forming a liquid base there, I regressed.

But there was one friend who was there for me unlike any other. Brad Chen became to me a friend beyond comparison.

Two to three times a week, we would escape from the world and retreat to his "upper room," where we would play something called Warhammer 40k, a glorified chess game that was our hobby. Countless hours were spent talking about the cares of life, sharing our hearts, and always dreaming. We would talk about girls, sports, and anything that came to mind. Up there, away from the world, we became the captain of our ships once again, and in our controlled environment, we found solitude and happiness.

We were the great generals that we knew we could be, and no disease nor any problems at home could find their places there. We sought peace, and amidst the endless hours of painting the Warhammer miniatures and playing war games, we learned how to communicate our feelings of despair coupled with a joy that was unshakable. Still, between "turns," I would inevitably have to run downstairs to the bathroom, trying to hide my shame all over again. Brad, as the true friend he was, never said anything and always supported me with an understanding love. He was a great friend.

My entire sophomore year in high school was spent trying to cope with a disease that ruled my life. No longer was I able to play the sports that God had gifted me with the ability to play. Soccer was out of the question, and baseball was hard to play as well, since I would be seen running to the port-o-potties almost every inning.

You see, I never knew when I would have to go to the bathroom, and it always seemed to be at the most inopportune times. The only sport that I could play was golf, since there were usually plenty of bushes to hide my shame, so I concentrated on that and became a good little golfer.

Midway through my sophomore year I started getting used to the disease that made me go to the bathroom almost twenty times a day. I soon forgot what it was like to stand up to go to the bathroom, and having a solid bowel movement was seen as an absolute gift from God. Never will I take for granted something so simple as having a solid bowel movement. Often times throughout the year I would hear people complain about having diarrhea for three days or a week, and I would shrug it off in my mind.

"If they only knew," is what I used to say.

Going to the movies was a different thing altogether for me, since I would inevitably have to go to the bathroom twice in the movie, and I would always have to see it a second time in order to get the whole story.

Life was difficult for me since I experienced extreme amounts of pain every day. I was losing weight fast, and the nutrients from foods were not going into my system as they should be. I was constantly fatigued from the amount of blood I was losing in my stools, and every social event was marred with the possibility of going to the bathroom in my pants.

As a sixteen-year-old, going to the bathroom in your pants is a humiliating thing, and I don't care what age you are, it rips you from your pride in a degrading way. Many people I have talked with ask, "But Daniel, I don't understand. You haven't done anything to deserve any of this, especially at such a young age."

But herein lies the point I am trying to make in this chapter: I haven't done anything to deserve any of this, but again, it was given to me that I may become a better man. Now, those words were given to me a long time ago, and in them I found no comfort. How can anyone say, "Daniel, your pain is for your own good." What kind of sadistic God would come up with such a plan for one of His kids? But I found that truth only after time, only after I saw what I had become and what I am becoming because of it.

I know that some people go through trials because of stuff that they have done to their own bodies, like alcoholism, drugs, sex, or a multitude of other things, but this trial in my life was to show that God has a sovereign, perfect plan for each one of us. It may have nothing to do with the lifestyle that we are leading, and it may have no source as to where it comes from, but nonetheless, God is glorified.

I see that now, having gone through something like this, something like a colon disease where my entire large intestine is one big ulcer and I go to the bathroom twenty times a day. There is no reason for it, and I can't comprehend any reason for it. But I trust in the Lord, since I have no other plan to trust in save my own, and that never comes to fruition, anyway. I have to embrace God's Lordship, as do we all, and again, realize my weakness.

We also must realize that we don't deserve anything, but that is something that I will get to later on in the book. But I am able to see now why God asked me to go through that trial, for it was all to His glory.

Can God be good still, amidst all the pain and suffering? How can I say that He is good still? I remember cheering in a high school volleyball game one time. It was late into the evening and my vocal chords were nearly shot. The gymnasium was hot with electricity and heat from the bodies on the court, coupled with the mass amounts of cheering fans screaming their lungs out. The girls playing volleyball were giving their all, and the fans were spurring them on to give more. I had a crush on one of the volleyball players at the time, though my self-esteem was destroyed, or rather, "in the toilet," because of the previously story shared.

As I said, it was late in the evening, and the girls needed to score one more point to win the game, and the fans were on edge.

The serve went up, propelled over the net and was returned in usual fashion. Two hits to make ready for the slam came quickly, and the spike came with crashing force.

Victory! I bolted from my seat in excitement and ran down on the court. Out of the corner of my eye, one of my bigger friends (and when I say bigger, I mean big) rushed towards me with much enthusiasm and grabbed hold of me. He raised me above his head and squeezed me; I let out a cry, and it happened. Oh, God, not again.

"Quick, let me down! Let me down!" With a confused look, he lowered me slowly. I had lost control of my bowels and had defecated in my pants right there on the court. My mind raced. *What should I do?* There was something like a revolution going on in that gymnasium, so everyone was going to see what Dan had done. My lips quivered. *Not now, God, please!*

I shot to the bathroom, my home away from home, and felt with each step more of a release from my bowels. No matter how hard I tried to hold it in, because of the disease, my body was forcing the contents of my bowels out and didn't care how fast. By the time I made it to the bathroom stall, some of the stools crept their way down to my socks, and I was utterly soiled. A couple people saw me jolt to the bathroom and followed me in. *What was I going to tell them? Did they see anything?*

This was my high school life from my sophomore year on; this was my curse. I found no meaning in what was happening to me, though people tried to tell me their own meaning they found vicariously through my pain. "What doesn't kill you makes you stronger." "This will make you into a better person."

Thanks, but I would gladly give this cup of suffering up, even for one day.

I sat there in the bathroom for two hours, and after I was sure no one was around, I peeked out, with streaks of tears down my eyes, and ran to my car. I had cleaned myself in the bathroom as well as I could with the limited amount of toilet paper that was available and lost myself in my tears.

I daydreamed again, of better days, as if I never had a disease like this. Shame was engulfing me slowly, as the tide creeps up on the shore. I wished in my dreams that pain was not to be found, that there was no such thing as the need to go to the bathroom, that each person would give me an understanding smile and that I would not be riddled with the fear that overwhelmed every member of my body.

My car lumbered into the driveway and I turned off the engine. After I did my best to clean up the car seat that was now a little soiled from the residuals of my earlier mess, I put my head in my hands and wept.

Thankfully, it was near midnight and both of my parents were asleep, so I went inside and washed myself in a warm shower. I was home, and I was safe. Safe from the uncertain glances, safe from the torturous and exhausting life that I was leading. Safe from the lack of control I found every day. Safe in the arms of an understanding family, and safe from myself. Safe.

LEARNING

I think security is really all we long for; security in self, security in finances, security in love, and security in God. Nowadays, to be in control is a virtue, and when our worlds get shaken, when our faith is brought to question, we assume the role of captain. We not only long for security in finances and such, but we desire security in relationships as well. But even in this idea of "security" there is more than a hint of utter selfishness. As I desired this concept more than a little at my relatively young age, amidst a torrent of emotional insecurity as well, I found myself dwelling within the confines of my own mind. My idea of security was based on what I saw around me, and those surrounding images influenced me.

So many of us try to find security in the wrong things. That is the problem with my generation and, unfortunately, all generations living and breathing today. We put so much effort in retirement plans, so much effort on the hope of pseudo controlled futures.

I vested my security in the desire to control my bowels, yet I realize now that it was no different than most people. Whether young or old, most people living today—myself included sometimes—think that they can actually attain control. We are so deceived in going about our busy days, living our own personal biographies out in relative ease and placing an almost virtuous importance on control and security.

This is such a huge shift from what we know and hear from the words of Jesus Himself. Yet, most of us again try to mix our own standards with the standards of righteousness and vest our hope in things that will ultimately perish. I am using Christian terms when I say perish, but we put so much emphasis on the things that will not last.

This is nothing new; this is not some shard of light into our consciences. We have all heard this before from the pulpits and from our Bible readings. But my Jesus, our Jesus, was and is radical and calls us to radically see things in a different light. Again, we must wake up from our lives, from the daydreams we are living, and step into the knowledge that is right in front of our faces.

Security, actual security, can only be seen in the correct way in light of Jesus and what He offers. There is no security outside our Christ, outside the God who came down here to die for us. Nothing else in all of creation can offer us the same incredible gift that shouts to our senses. *"Wake up,"* He screams. *"You gather like ants and don't see the shoe above you."* Our only security is in the loving God who wears that shoe. The God we serve has laced that shoe tightly and is striding towards our hope, giving us a reason to believe and a reason to find security. Such is the awful yet holy perception we must have of our God. So many of us who have some misconstrued view of our Creator believe that the shoe is indeed coming down on us, when in fact, it is protecting us from terrible raindrops of destruction.

Our security, in radical terms, is found in the Lord. God gives and takes away, but blessed be His name, for in His perfect plan, He has total control. Total control is in the hands of a God who knows all and has perfect wisdom.

I don't know about most of you, but none of my plans that I had for my life have turned out, and I praise God for that. For in that scary reality of my perfect plan lies the awesome reality of my certain destruction. Yet, God, in His spectacular grace, has saved me from my own pathetic plans and lifted me up with His. Do I deserve the things He has blessed me with? Absolutely not, and neither do any of the rest of us. So I, and all of us for that matter, would do well to trust in the God who has labeled all securities in our lives and perfectly controls our destinies.

Listen to the words of Jesus that so many of us take for granted:

"Therefore I tell you, do not worry about your life, what you will eat or drink; or about your body, what you will wear. Is not life more important than food, and the body more important than clothes? Look at the birds of the air; they do not sow or reap or store away in barns, and yet your heavenly Father feeds them. Are you not much more valuable than they? Who of you by worrying can add a single hour to his life? And why do you worry about clothes? See how the lilies of the field grow. They do not labor or spin. Yet I tell you that not even Solomon in all his splendor was dressed like one of these. If that is how God clothes the grass of the field, which is here today and tomorrow is thrown into the fire, will He not much more clothe you, O you of little faith? So do not worry, saying, 'What shall we eat?' or 'What shall we drink?' or 'What shall we wear?' For the pagans run after all these things, and your heavenly Father knows that you need them. But seek first His kingdom and His righteousness, and all these things will be given to you as well. Therefore, do not worry about tomorrow, for tomorrow will worry about itself. Each day has enough trouble of its own" (Matthew 6.25–34).

My generation is a generation to hear these words and pass them off as impossible. "Christ's words are not relevant for today," some may say, for they do not see nor can they comprehend "something out there" controlling our most intimate of moments and realities. I will say that Jesus is radical over and over again, for I believe that in light of the presuppositions of today, His teachings are so contrary to how we actually live out our days. How much does not worrying about tomorrow, "for each day has enough trouble of its own," completely contradict all that we learn from television and the cinema? If we look at our lives and the rituals we go through each day, we can see correctly that we are creatures of habit, trying to "get" the next great thing, vesting security in something created.

All of this is stemmed, and I believe most "Christians" live this way as well, from an incorrect placement of the Lord as Lord. No longer is Jesus Christ Lord of our lives, respected and holy, but instead, we treat him as a Santa Claus we pull out of our pockets; hidden, only brought out when we desperately need something. We do not let him be Lord, and such is the sorry state in which we often find ourselves. When God no longer reigns as King in our lives, we become the masters of our own destinies and feel that control should be within our grasp. And when control slips through our fingers, as it does everyday, we worry and don't put our trust in God.

We have such a misconstrued idea of God and how He works in our lives. Hence we have such a misconstrued idea of how control is gained and lost. When I was younger, living out my days in a pain amplifier whenever I visited the toilet, I searched for control and found nothing within my grasp. When we are honest with ourselves as the created, we realize that we can only see dimly through a "keyhole" that we actually have no control. We must accept this, for it is imperative to living radically for Jesus.

We have to wake up out of our daydreams and realize that, ultimately, we have no control. Who can explain the pain in our lives, or who can explain the loss of life that is so rampant throughout the history of the world? No one can, and no matter how hard we try, we can do nothing about it. We are not the masters of our own destinies as so many of us hope. We can live as healthy as possible, eat the right things, do the right things, but ultimately, we cannot control the day we die.

The plan for our lives has already been ordained, we are only living out our novels, reaching closer to the last page with the passing of each day. This is such a gloomy view of reality, but something with which I am all too familiar. With all of my pain and trials, with all of my health issues, I am not guaranteed more than fifteen years from now. I firmly believe that the doctors are wrong, but ultimately, all I can do is rely on the God who created me. I am not even guaranteed tomorrow, but all of us feel as though we are.

I once read about a man who was diagnosed with a very rare cancer. His doctors told him his death was only months away. He went home incredibly sad. He resolved to not die in the hospital bed, but to live life to its fullest with the wife he loved so desperately.

Once the shock of death wore off, if it could ever do so, they planned their first vacation together. After months of travel and intentional time spent as a couple, they sat down on their living room couch and prayed together. After that, they spent hours together for the next couple of days, talking and loving each other like never before.

It was the most precious time they had ever had, and they grew even more deeply in love. Each word they spoke was shadowed by his looming death, but was lightened because of his eternal security. You see, he was a Christian and loved Jesus with all of his heart.

The wife knew this, too, and knew the God whom they served and on whose love they founded their marriage. After a few more weeks had passed, this couple began sowing into their community, vesting their legacy into the youth with which they came in contact.

After the projected date of death had passed, the man, with death firmly accepted and planted in his mind, went into the hospital to have another diagnosis. He found that the doctors had been wrong all along and that there wasn't a trace of cancer in his body.

Sheer joy went through his body and sent him bolting for the door to tell his wife, who was alone in the waiting room.

Standing there together, embraced in love, they made a pact to continue to live their lives as if each one was dying of cancer. For in that truth of not being in control, they lived with more joy and compassion and were happier than they had ever been before.

I am not advocating such a morbid view on life, but giving up control into the hands of the One who created us would be an incredible step towards living how we actually are called to live. "*Do not worry about tomorrow . . .*" God is in control, not you, so, please, stop living as if you were. He has a much better and much bigger plan for our lives than we could possibly imagine, and having faith in a God who has chosen us to live with Him in eternity is no bad thing. In fact, it is imperative to living a life of freedom and ultimately a life of perfect control. When we give our lives to God, when we give up the freedom of saying this or that for our lives, when we give up control, He gives it back to us and provides miraculously in such incredible ways. Give Him control of your life, and watch Him provide . . .

"That is all well and good," you may say, "but I can't exactly sink my teeth into that truth when in the midst of a confusing trial." How do we come to that truth—that God is indeed in control—when we are going through extreme heartache? As we attempt to contemplate God's truths amidst our trials, what are the words that can offer any hope, any rest, any security? What kind of a God would allow seemingly heartless acts of terror or pain and somehow offer no explanation? Is that the "loving" God anyone would want to serve? That makes no sense, for we have all been brought up to believe in this loving Creator who cares for us enough to die for us. The dichotomy of a loving God who stands back and allows certain pain in our lives does not sit well with us.

It truly is excruciatingly difficult to grasp in our finite minds. What do you say to someone who just had a loved one die, or someone who was just diagnosed with a rare disease? "*Take courage, your God, the God, has a perfect plan and will see you through*"? How heartless, how terrible, and how confusing that would be. On one hand, we serve this God who personally provides for us in everything, and on the other hand, we see a God that stretches us beyond the limits of our own sanity at times. We pull our hair, we stay up late at night in stress, we even sometimes deny this idea of God since our own plans seem to not come to fruition. After all, we believe that we know better, and that if we were in control, we wouldn't allow this to happen to us. If we were God, our plans would be of peace and rest, with lamb lying with lion, with Iraqi brothers playing checkers with American soldiers. That makes sense, doesn't it? That is logical, isn't it? On one hand, yes; on the other, absolutely not. Yet many of us are not able to hear, for we do not even have the ears to do so. We don't even have the eyes to see nor to contemplate the grand design of a wonderful Creator.

Yet here we sit, on our sofas, on our couches or Lazy-boys, easily angered by the storms around us. *"Why doesn't God intervene more often in our lives?"* Why didn't God intervene and heal me of this ter- *rible disease that offered me many expedited trips to the toilet? Why did He allow it in the first place?* I can't tell you how many times I asked those very questions from the spot described, on that porcelain seat, with my trousers covered in stools. But inevitably, as I think back on it now, and as I have asked that question thousands of times since, God boldly yells to me in return, "Who are you that I should answer?"

But if God is so personal, wouldn't it make sense that He would indeed answer us? If He would send His own Son to die a grue- some death on our behalf, wouldn't it follow that He would gladly answer our petitions like some radio jockey that we call into for questions? Is that the character of God, is that consistent with His holy character?

Let me give you a terrible example that doesn't do this argument justice but may shed a spectacle of light. Put yourself in the position of someone who had to answer for President Bush during a time of great ridicule. Let's just say that President Bush had just given a lecture in San Francisco; an area known to hold and express extreme liberal views. There would no doubt be many questions after the lecture.

Now, I am not asking you to think like a conservative or take sides in any political arena, but I am asking you to imagine with me for a second. What would those questions be like, say, during the War with Iraq? Most of the questions would be in the form of insults, but the source of those questions would be from everyday people like you and me. Most people would ask intensely personal questions directly involving them. In their confusion, they would expect an answer. Would you expect President Bush to answer *all* of the personal questions, or rather, would you even feel that he would need to? Most of the questions themselves would have little, if any, relevance to the big picture, yet, from the vantage-point of the inquirer, would seem of utmost importance. Those questions are very myopic and focus on a very small portion of the overarching plan.

God, in His extreme and perfect love does not answer questions that don't need answering. This is not insensitivity, nor is it wrong. Job, in his dire need amidst incredible loss that most of us will never face, asked God a similar question. In effect, he said, "Where are You? Why are You allowing these terrible things to happen to me? I have done nothing wrong." In God's perfect reply, something that still should shake us to our cores, responds, "No Job, *who* are *you*? Do you think you can understand my ways? I am God, not you. I know what is best for my glory and for my redemptive plan; not you."

So I ask you, instead of asking so many questions to a God that provides all the control we ever could need, who are you that God should reply? Are you the most important thing on this planet, or is the God who controls everything? Many of us think so highly of ourselves that we believe even the God of creation has to answer to us. And when He doesn't, when He seemingly "ignores" our truly heartfelt but suggestive questions, we grow angry because our finite plans are not carried out to fruition. Can you at least see how incredibly absurd that is and how amazingly high and lifted up we have put ourselves, that even God, who is grander than the stars, should be at our beck and call?

God is indeed in control of our lives, and if God is God, which He is, we should see Him as thus.

alone

It was noon, and we had just been released for lunch. I was walking to my locker in a daze. It was my junior year now, my colon disease was finally under control somewhat, and I was buzzing with my other friends as to where I might want to go to college.

As we walked amidst the crowd of students and made our way to the cafeteria line, I bumped into someone I hadn't seen for a couple of weeks, for it was a very large school of over three thousand. He said to me, "Dan, whoa, are you some kind of freak? What is wrong with your eyes? Why are they so yellow?"

Putting my hands in my pocket and gazing at the ground in search of an answer that might suffice, I told him that I wasn't feeling well. I knew exactly what was ailing me, but I didn't want to face it. I had already gone through so much pain with my large intestine disease and didn't want to face this new dilemma.

I was two days seventeen now and running from something. Running from fear of the unknown, running from being different again, and running from those types of questions that pierced my heart and destroyed my spirit. As he was waiting for an answer, my vision became blurry and I started losing my composure. With watery eyes, I shocked my poor innocent friend with one swift reply.

"I am dying of a liver disease, and my eyes are jaundice."

That is quite a lot of information to load onto someone who was expecting an altogether different reply.

We tend to not think about the questions we ask when something is out of the norm, out of the ordinary and out of our comfort zone, not realizing the hurt that we may be implying. I know that my friend did not have malicious intentions, for I have had conversations with him since, but my answer was rooted from a sense of exhaustion at the amount of times I was asked the same question. Being on the side of the questioning, being on the end where people don't know how to react to what you represent, is a sobering experience. It has given me compassion for those who are hurting, a sense that I know what someone is going through when people stare.

My eyes were, without a doubt, clearly yellow, and people would often take two or even three glances to make sure that they saw correctly. I was dying of a liver disease, and dying quickly. I was seventeen years old, and I faced the reality that I had months to live. Such was the reality that I awoke to each morning as I crawled out of bed. No matter how hard I tried to escape, I would always find my way back to the haunting truth of disease and death knocking on my soul.

One morning, a few weeks prior to that incident on the high school campus, my mother noticed something in my eyes. I can't imagine how she must have felt as she tried to hide the inevitable when I looked at her that morning, oblivious to the fact that something serious was wrong. Maybe I chose not to notice my eyes each morning as I looked in the mirror, for I didn't want to worry about the possibility of something being wrong. I so desperately wanted to live a "normal" life, filled with the average, everyday trials that go with the territory of being an adolescent. But I was confronted that morning with a pained look in my mother's eyes as she asked for me to draw closer to her that she might have a better look. As concern filled my mother's eyes, she quickly called my doctor and scheduled an appointment to figure out what might be wrong.

Hoping against hope, I visited my colon doctor, who now was a close friend, and he scheduled a time for me to get diagnosed through a procedure to analyze my liver. For a week, I walked around school trying to concentrate on what was directly ahead of me, not the unstable future of what could be. But the looming questions seemed to invade my soul and penetrate every facet of my being. It was as if a cloud had enveloped me and I was walking alone in a fog of uncertainty. It's where I never wanted to fully deal with the immediate but also didn't want to live in the paranoid future of a thousand possibilities. I remember distinctly talking with friends during lunch and not being myself, having every silent moment steal me from the realm of high school into the realm of something unfamiliar.

The time came for my diagnosis, and with a fearful eagerness, I was given the drugs to silence my mind and numb my senses. Precious lies of comfort from others convinced me that everything was going to be alright. Waking up in the middle of the procedure with tubes down my throat and vivid images of the doctor yelling for more medication seemed to burn its home in my memories, but even more indelible was the news that I was indeed dying.

The doctor told me after the procedure, with both parents seated on the recovery bed with me, that I had a disease called Primary Sclerosis Cholangitis, PSC, and that I was in dire need of another liver.

A liver transplant—the second biggest surgery known to man at that point—is what my future held.

Tears formed in his eyes and fell to the floor, my parents' and mine both joining his into a puddle on the linoleum. Faced with the very real possibility of death, I did what any other kid would have done—I ignored it and wished it away.

As hard as I could, I desired balance in my life, and for three years straight, I had found only chaos. Claiming ignorance was the easy way out for me; it became the mask for my fear, and people soon began to recognize it as strength. But those encounters with my friends, those times when people would stare at my eyes for a little longer than what I deemed comfortable, quickly shot me back to the reality that I was indeed different, and that I was indeed dying.

By the end of November, which was within two months of my diagnosis, I was feeling the effects of my disease in full force. I was sleeping up to fifteen hours a day, my legs retained water so much that I could squeeze my ankles and leave imprints, my stomach became severely bloated, my skin was affected by long-term jaundice and became yellow as well as itching uncontrollably and my energy level was reduced to nothing. I was destroyed physically, mentally and spiritually, and I saw myself affected more and more each day.

I remember the day that I was finally put on the waiting list—December 22, 1995. I was given a beeper that would tell me when a liver was ready for me.

At that time, organs were needed to be transplanted within a certain amount of time lest the organ itself die from lack of oxygen and other complications.

A day and a half later, as I was walking up the steps late to a Christmas service at my church, I received a page from my mother. From my mother! *Didn't she know that the hospital was supposed to be paging me and that I would have a heart attack when I found her number listed instead of the hospital's?* She wasn't supposed to be doing that, but grudgingly, I figured she was probably just testing it.

Adrenaline was rushing through my veins as a result of the momentary thought that this page meant there was a liver available for me. Much to my disappointment, however, I was quickly let down when I realized it was my mother calling. After dialing my home number, I heard one ring on the phone.

"Hello?"

"Mom, why did you page me?"

"Danny," with tears so loud in her voice that they could almost be heard audibly through the phone lines, "they have found a liver for you. You are going to live!"

Tears still form in my mind whenever I think about that phone call and have formed even now as I type. It was such a powerful statement, for I had been living in misery for two months, and the prospect of death quickly vanished.

Hope was reborn in one phone conversation. Death would not be the answer.

I can remember saying goodbye to my mother; she made me promise that I wouldn't drive home lest something happen to me and asked me to get someone else to take me instead. Walking down the aisle of the church, I talked to the main pastor of my five thousand-member-church, and they corporately prayed for me. All my friends followed me home and a remnant of them, around twenty or so, followed me the forty miles to the hospital so they could be there in support.

That drive was incredible. What do you talk about? What do you say? I was going to live, but I now faced that for which I had hardly any time to prepare, a major surgery that was certain to leave me devastated for months. The entire car ride to the hospital was spent mostly in silence, mostly in complete praise and adoration to a God that was only beginning to test my love and faith for Him. It was a car ride easily overlooked, but hardly forgotten.

Some incredible things happened to me in the form of God's blessings while I was in the hospital. For one, I was released ten days post-operation, which was unheard of. I hardly had time to collect my thoughts on the matter since I was out for four of those ten days from the amount of morphine in my system. But something that needs to be mentioned, before I go any further, is the absurdity of my wait time for receiving a liver transplant. I once heard the statistic from a study done in 1994 that over fifty thousand people a year die from not getting the organs needed for transplantation. I received mine within a day and a half, and to this day, no doctor has ever heard of anything like that ever happening.

Some people call that luck, but with Christ as the filter for my worldview, I see it as a divine miracle. It was later speculated that I had weeks to live because the disease had hit me so hard. But the seriousness of the disease was never fully actualized because of the transplant.

There were many other provisions that God blessed me with in those days that I was in and out of the hospital. I was blessed to never need a blood transfusion during or following the surgery, so I never had to worry about possible complications from that. I had an extra tube in my liver, something that they are never able to salvage from the dead, and so was able to forgo other complicated surgeries. Normally, with most liver transplants during that time, the doctors would have to put a plastic tube in a main liver duct and have it protrude outside the body, only to remove it weeks later with another surgery and hospital stay. I was able to bypass this extra step miraculously. I also didn't have to take drugs intravenously for the projected hundred days; only thirty two. It was as if God said, "Dan, I am going to make this as easy on you as possible."

But one night, as I lay in that hospital bed all alone, with the screams of other patients being clearly heard and understood, I was forced to deal with something that I didn't want to deal with. You see, my mother had just told me previously that hour that my own father, the one person I respected more than anyone, was leaving the house. My parents were getting a divorce.

I often think back on that time of my life and wonder how on earth I ever was able to deal with it. And that is the thing; I know that I can't even handle it when someone makes me angry because of their ignorance, so how much less can I handle a liver transplant and the divorce of my parents at the same time? God's strength was manifested through me, and that is my answer. I have to give Him all of the glory.

I know that it was not my strength, because when I arrived home from the hospital, eager to finally spend Christmas together as a family, my mother pulled the car into the driveway and with a loud thump, we stopped. She inadvertently ran over my favorite cat—if one can have a cat be their favorite—and opened the floodgates of tears down my face. I guess I needed something to project my feelings onto or something, but it was the straw that broke my back. I wept and wept, partly because the medication was affecting my feelings, and I became so sad that day because a stupid cat died. You can probably imagine how terrible my mother must have felt, but without going into much detail at this moment, she was my angel. Without her pointing me towards always seeking God, I never would have made it through. Though suicide was never an option for me and I never thought about it, I can only speculate the feelings I might have had without my mother guiding me. She is a messenger from Heaven sent to encourage me and give me joy. I love her.

We have had so many bonding moments together, but none so strong as the following months and into my senior year of high school. After twenty-nine years of marriage, my father was divorcing my mother, and every night I heard her down the hall bawling herself to sleep. Countless nights were spent trying to drown out the noises of the one person who was supposed to be my rock, countless nights numbing the pain in my ears and countless times feeling like going crazy because of the torturous moans that she battled into the night. There were times that I would wake up in the middle of the night, only to stop in the hallway and hear that she was still crying at three o'clock in the morning. Her world came crashing down, and with that, my back began to stiffen. I became harder because my mother became softer.

DAYDREAM

My feet were raw from the constant running I was doing, yet, my muscles were not tired. I could see the salt in the air as it whispered its way towards me. No one was active on the beach that day, for the sky was overcast—something that happened all too often. The string in my hands grew taught as I released more of the line to the kite. I looked around me and found no one. I was alone, yet, something was out of the ordinary. Why was I suddenly on the beach all by myself? Where was everyone? My chest was pounding from all of the running I had been doing, and I vaguely remembered holding someone's hand, but now, no one was near.

I pushed the thought of aloneness out of my head and concentrated on the task at hand. I was seventeen now, and I didn't need to worry about where mom was. I knew my brothers were gone, for I hadn't spent too much time with them recently, anyway.

Seagulls—one almost broke my line to the kite that suddenly was so important to me. A flock of seagulls (wasn't that a band name?) completely enshrouded my kite, tearing it to pieces. I reeled it in as quickly as possible, but before I could withdraw ten yards worth, my shredded kite came tumbling to the ground. Now what?

The sand suddenly felt coarse between my toes, and, all in one instant, the sun burned away the layer of fog that kept me covered. This day was weird. What was happening to me? Why are no people on the beach?

Now that my kite was destroyed, what else did I have left to do?

Sand. I can build sandcastles.

But I am seventeen years old; seventeen-year-olds don't build sand castles.

I bent down to form some of the wet sand into a mound, when I was suddenly struck with the feeling of hopelessness and helplessness. Why was there no one to experience this beautiful day with me? Why was I so alone? With that last question, I stood up and raced down the beach some more. Completely clean and white beaches stretched as far as the eye could see, and far into the distance, a dock pierced the already wondrous coastline.

The sun burned a hole into my back as I screamed to deafen the silence, taunting all to hear. Falling down into the soft, wet sand, I lost myself in the image of a sand dollar, broken to pieces. For some reason, I felt as though I could relate to that sand dollar. I was half broken myself, and I felt so alone on this beach, surrounded by millions of grains of sand.

CONTINUED DREAM

No longer naïve to the ideality of people, I developed a hate for my father and a distrust of all of those around me. I learned later that year the real reason my father was divorcing my mother, or at least the real reason why reconciliation was impossible to reach.

My father says that he didn't start his relationship with the other woman, a good twenty three years younger than him, until he served my mother her divorce papers. My mother still claims to this day that this wasn't true, that the adulterous affair began prior to the serving of the divorce papers, but the fact is he began another relationship with a woman who wasn't my mother—one that was younger than my oldest brother's wife.

It was a quick one-two punch from the enemy, and it was devastating. Though I didn't allow anyone to know the severity of the impact it was having on me—so I could still be the leader in the high school group at church, so I could still be ASB Vice President of my student body—I was becoming hollow inside. Unforgiveness was eating at me with an insatiable appetite, and I was becoming a very bitter person.

My mother noticed this, and, early in my senior year, she got down on her knees to petition to the Lord on my behalf. She became a prayer warrior, for it was in that prayer that she found her strength. She connected with God and so started down the healing process that was imperative for her. But my healing did not come, nor could it come, until I had an encounter with God. That encounter did not come until five years later.

LEARNING

One of the greatest philosophies that permeates our senses is this hope in something out there in Space. We have such a belief that we are not the only ones in creation, for our senses tell us that outer Space is too grand, too expansive to not house some other form of creation. This all stems from the fact that we don't want to be alone because being alone is a terrible thing. I am not talking about marriage, for that great and holy institution is profaned daily. But when I say alone, I am referring to a concept of understanding. There are two forms of loneliness that we so desperately run from yet yearn to fill everyday.

We are alone as created beings, able to think logically with coherency, and we are alone in our trials when no one around us is going through the same thing. Look at Hollywood and the writers of so many science fiction movies . . . we long for something out there that can relate to us as human beings. The fame of Star Wars and Star Trek alone is evidence of this. But if we were to look intently into the awesome grandeur of God Himself, we would see in obvious truth that the "*Heavens declare the glory of God and the skies proclaim the work of His hands*" (Psalm 19.1). If the heavens do indeed declare, shout, and proclaim God's glory, then it would be obvious that the huge expansiveness of the stars shows us plainly that God is bigger and more awesome than anything we could ever imagine.

When you look up at the stars, viewing the big and little dippers, do you see constellations and end your thought with those alone? Or do you see the fingerprints of a God who is so majestic and overwhelming that even the expanse of the stars speaks of His wonder? Instead of seeing God as an entity that is out there and uncaring, hence us being alone and feeling alone, we would do well to look at the universe as it really is—speaking of His glory and showing us an incredible God on one hand, and a personal God who intimately fashions us from our mother's womb on the other. Such is the astonishingly wonderful God I serve.

Post modern thought has done away with this idea that there is something out there that we can connect to, but amidst the pain of trials, we feel so alone and long for someone, something to let us know that there is someone who understands. How many people are constantly saying that they are "spiritual" beings, connecting with a form of god but not really God at all? In the empty chambers of their own minds they "need" to connect with something, to not feel so alone.

I am reminded now of a line in *Braveheart* when one of William Wallace's comrades was making a spectacle of himself because he was talking with God out loud in front of everyone else. He said,

"In order to find an equal, an Irishman is forced to talk to God . . . yes Father, I'll tell them . . ." And I won't quote the rest because of obscene language. But my point is that when I see the faces of students walking around colleges, I see a loneliness that doesn't need to be there.

This feeling of being alone is put in exponential terms when going through life-threatening or horrendous trials. "No one could possibly understand what I am going through because no one else has been through what I am dealing with" This is something I hear all of the time. But that is a lie that consumes us.

Like walking zombies, oblivious to the fact that we serve a radical God, we don't see Jesus' words as radical. The word *radical* gives us a glimpse of understanding what God is really like. In this concept of being alone, look at God in light of the word "radical." He *is* so huge, majestic, and abundant, with His glory being clearly seen in the expansiveness of the universe. He *is* so holy, and calls us to be so as well. But His character doesn't stop there, and so many of us lose our footing on this alone.

God is radical and isn't logical in almost any sense of the word. He is wholly different than anything we could ever imagine, and that makes me fall on my knees in worship, even amidst the pain of a liver transplant. Since God is perfect, holy, and unfathomable, it makes no sense that He is incredibly personal as well. But He *is*, for He sent His own Son to die for us. *That* is radical love, and what is more, personal love. We are not alone, for the universe was created for us and us alone, that we might see the glory of God. For when we recognize His glory, we fall down and worship this God who came down to die for us. In a sense, this idea of the universe created for our viewing is definitely homocentric, but not when it allows us to recognize the Creator. He wants to be recognized by His greatest creation. He cares for us that much.

Yet we feel alone still, for this idea of God does not sit well with some of us. With others this fits in great, for we put ourselves truly in the center of the universe.

"How many blondes does it take to screw in a light bulb? One, she

stands in the room holding the light bulb and the world revolves around her . . ."

Many of us have heard and often repeated this ridiculous joke, but that is how we see ourselves. But if the argument stands, if God is indeed that personal, which He is, then how does that offer any hope amidst our trials? It does because God not only loves us, but He understands the things we go through.

"What could Christ possibly know about a liver transplant?" Sounds like a very valid question when you think about it, since transplantation didn't exactly happen back then, but the truth in the question gives away its absurdity. Or take for example, cancer and all that is associated with that terrible disease. Does Christ know *that* kind of suffering, *that* kind of pain? When people ask those questions, they are asking to raise a checklist, scar-list or whatever else you may call it, which lists plainly the trials each person has been through. I did this, and I took pride in my scar list later on in life, but when we raise that list, we must not be blind to the list Christ can raise. Long after we have checked off each specific pain and trial, we can see that Christ's list goes on.

Sometimes, to know that we are not alone in our trials, to know in our minds that there is someone who understands and even cares, it is good to be reminded of Christ's pain—His checklist of pain, if you will.

Though it is very graphic, I will spare no details, for shock is sometimes needed for things to sink in with us. Jesus, beaten with leather straps that had iron balls attached to the ends so that they would rip his skin literally apart, was then handed over to government soldiers for mock ridicule and crazy insults. As if the pain of the whipping was not enough, the soldiers robbed Him of his clothes and dignity, leaving him almost naked for all to see, and put on Him a royal red robe, screaming doubt into His ears. What could that have been like, when all of His closest friends had left Him and He didn't have one friendly face to offer any encouragement or peace?

Encircled with enemies left and right shouting and threatening Him, Jesus was given a crown of thorns, similar to a barbed-wire fence. They shoved it around the top of His head, obviously scratching the skull, maybe even the actual bone. My brother once had a nurse accidentally hit a bone in his arm while giving him a shot, and he told me shakily that it was the most painful thing he had ever experienced. I can't imagine what it would feel like to have something like that scraping the inside of my skin, digging deep and crunching on bone. In the middle of all this pain and turmoil—when I, for one, would be yelling, no, screaming my breath away to be released—Jesus stood there, in the middle of the angry soldiers, and received the blows.

Perhaps the most disgusting thing that happened during that ridicule was the fact that they "spat on Jesus." Those filthy soldiers probably mixed their saliva with other things like mucus and such, spitting directly into the open wounds of Christ. Stop and think about that for a second. Put this book down and realize how disgusting that sight must have been. Picture blood mixed with spit and mucous-filled saliva dripping down His back. Please excuse me for being so graphic, but let that image burn in your minds the next time you think that your pain is much worse than anything Christ could have been through. Think about the saliva when you feel alone, as if no one knows what you are going through. How is your checklist holding up right now? Mine stopped a couple of sentences ago.

Allow me to continue, though the vulgarity will stop, I promise. After they had spit on Jesus, they then took a stick, equal to something you would walk with on a hike, and beat him on the head. It must have been hemorrhaging as the assailants beat Him over and over again, seemingly without a care for His human dignity. Matthew, the gospel writer that I am referring to, does not mention that they took the crown of thorns off before they began this separate beating, so don't lose that. If the crown was not permanently lodged around His temples before, it no doubt was after that flogging. Again, they stripped Him of His dignity, though I can't see Him caring at that point with the pain being more than excruciating, and put His own clothes on Him again and led Him away to be crucified (Matthew 27.26–31).

After all of this, they led our Christ up a path with him carrying a huge section of a wooden cross—His own instrument of death held firmly in His hands. How lonely was that path? Amidst the insurmountable pain that must have been throbbing in all areas of His body, and the noise of pulsing blood pounding in His mind and drowning out the cries of the people around Him, how lonely must He have felt? Almost all of His closest friends had abandoned Him to face this torment alone.

Then nails, huge spiked pieces of iron, were driven through His joints with a large mallet, that He might be held up high on the cross (Matthew 27.32–50).

Finally, He died there on that cross, experiencing the most excruciating pain of all, suffocating and fighting for each breath until His last. How does your list compare with Jesus'?

Still, you may fight with the pathetic claim that Christ didn't suffer torment for very long compared to, say, your specific disease. But if you do compare, then *truly* compare, and marvel at what our Christ has gone through for us.

And there is one little thing that Christ has on His list that completely wipes away our loneliness and despair. Of course, it is written on the bottom of His list, so you might have missed it. It might read like this: "Risen from the dead, conquered sin, source of hope amidst your own pain . . ."

That gives me peace, that gives me hope, and that alone is what makes me feel like someone can relate to me. For all of that pain, all of that extreme heartache, was for me. Most of our trials happen to us because of circumstances outside of our control, but Christ chose that pain specifically so we wouldn't have to face it. He loves us that much. Now don't you think that He never wants us to feel alone?

running

i t was my freshmen year in college, and I had just stepped on campus. Point Loma Nazarene College, now University, was the farm where I cultivated my faith over the next two and a half years. The school itself is breathtaking—palm trees swaying in the slight breeze produced by the coast that is less than a hundred yards from the freshman dorms coupled with the most beautiful sunsets God has ever created. There is a peace on that campus that is hard to express, yet, I was dealing with my own personal war, one that raged violently within my mind.

All four years of high school were spent dealing with the traumas of my best friend's death, a colon disease that squelched my joy and sent shards of excruciating pain throughout the inner workings of my body, almost dying from a liver disease and ultimately getting a liver transplant, and dealing with the effects of a divorce. I was eager now to start a new life, a life that promised freedom from all of those bands that tied me to a history that would send anyone to their knees.

And so I began college, naïve to the fact that nothing was going to change, naïve to the fact that I couldn't escape the seriousness of what had happened to me, and desiring more than anything to run away, to live a normal life. My first days there were outstanding, in a word, for I forgot completely what had happened. I met new people who had their own stories, people who had no idea about my past, people who loved me despite what I had been through. One of those people was a student named Kelly. She was more beautiful than anything I could ever imagine, and she was in my orientation group.

I remember the first moment I saw her as she stepped down the stairs to meet with the group before we departed on our tour of the campus. With shyness, she projected her innocence and her beauty all the more, and I had to meet her. She would later become my companion who has now been with me for over nine years. Through the tumultuous life that I led, she stood by me every step of the way. It is to her that I have given my heart, and it is to her that I owe a good portion of my strength.

Our group was comprised of many eager freshmen about to partake on a grand experience of college, one promising many adventures and setbacks. A group filled with boyish grins and female confidence, with a certain idealism ready to be shattered. And my naïveté quickly fell to the floor in a slump later that first day as I was in Brown Chapel, a place where God was proclaimed.

Out of the corner of my eye—as most of the freshmen class sat through lectures on financial aid, not really listening but checking everyone else out–I saw my father come strolling down the aisle. You can imagine how I must have felt since my parents were supposed to have left earlier that day, and now I saw my father sympathetically staring at me. Seeing him motion me to come to him, I got up from my coveted seat next to Kelly and quickly went to him.

Without saying a word, I followed him to the back of the chapel and met my mother in tears.

Not again. Please, Lord, not again. Not this time, let me just have a breath, Lord, not again.

"Danny, I am sorry, but the results from your blood tests you took last week have come back. You are in chronic rejection."

"What? What does that mean?"

"Your body is rejecting your liver, and it is slowly destroying it."

Silence.

It was happening all over again. No matter how hard I tried, I couldn't get away from that disease. It had been almost a year since anything had gone wrong with my liver, since I had that terrible transplant, and right then and there I learned that I would have to deal with it the rest of my life.

Rage filled me. Questions aroused. *Why was this happening to me? Hadn't I been through enough already? What did this mean? Did this mean that I was going to have to have another transplant?* I would rather have died than go through another one. After a year's time, I was finally getting back to normal strength. A year! And now this. It felt as if I was running and no matter how hard I tried, the rubber bands that had attached like barbs to my back always whipped me, hurling me backwards to where I was running from. I couldn't break free from pain and trials. They had become a part of me, something like a plague that sent me searching the cosmos for answers. Like a wart that one tries cutting off themselves, the trials kept coming back no matter how deep I cut and no matter how much effort I put into it. I was devastated.

The following week, while everyone was going to their first classes and worrying about what they looked like and who they met, I spent my time driving to and from the hospital to get steroids pumped into me intravenously—steroids that exhausted me, steroids that ate away at my muscles and bones, steroids that ravaged me emotionally. After the week I spent doing that, I can remember sitting on my dorm room bed—with two other roommates in the room with me, ones that I did not know a single thing about—feeling more alone than ever.

Both of my parents had left me; I knew no one, and no one knew or had any idea what I was dealing with. I remember going to my R.A. and asking him to pray for me because I was scared that I was going to have to have another liver transplant. I remember going to the bathroom and taking showers, having to explain to everyone why my massive scars were there.

Scars. My scars. The scars that everyone balked at upon first reviewing with their unpretentious eyes. These scars became to me a tattoo, a meaning, a leech that attached itself to the outside of my skin with roots going deep within my soul. Hidden from plain sight by the covering of clothes, they held on to my psyche, ever twisting their tendrils to the tip-top of my brain. They had become a part of me, a friend, though one I at first hid in shame.

I remember a time when I went on a vacation to Palm Desert with my family after I had received my first transplant. As I walked out to the pool I saw that it was filled with many children. The thought of possibly having to explain my story to them, along with seeing the effects of the surgery in the visible staples present along my stomach, sent fear racing to clutch at my heart. With a humility and anxiety all my own, I lifted my shirt with my heart racing, dreading the looks and the onrush of questions. Thus began the story of my life whenever I raised a shirt, whenever I publicly went swimming, whenever I uncovered even a fraction of my stomach. And now, since college was filled with new spectators and eager young minds that want to bring meaning to whatever they see, I was riddled with questions upon naïve questions.

I can't blame them though, for I know that I do the same thing. I know that when something strikes me as out of the ordinary, out of the norm, my senses are overloaded and I want to find answers. Why are we like that? Why do we sacrifice sensitivity of others to fill our own selfish thoughts to find order and control? That question vexes me, though the answer is just that. We ask those questions; we need to find those answers regardless of who we hurt emotionally in the process, because we are what we are. Without philosophizing this too much, we are humans, and since we live for ourselves, we think only of ourselves. This is not an excuse; this is a dilemma. This is the plague that hinders us from leading free lives. This is the disease that yells, "Crucify Him!"

Though you may think this is a random interjection, I am deeply concerned with the way we interact with others who are in need of an ear, not an earful. In those dorm rooms and in those classrooms, I was drawn to people who knew how to listen, not the ones who boasted in their talking. I can remember sitting on my bed in tears, trying to find meaning to my constant suffering. The medication I was taking for my liver—because of the heightened need for certain effects to take place—did incredible damage to my large intestine. I say this with a sigh, for there is much pain in that statement. If you will remember, I had a large intestine disease that made the lining of my colon one big ulcer at times. Though I hadn't experienced any flare-ups for quite some time, the medication triggered it in a major way.

Coupled with dealing with a possible second liver transplant that I would rather die than have to repeat, I was slowly fading away from the extreme amount of bowel movements that I proceeded to have that year. Nights were filled with pain, as I would run, literally run, to the bathroom in hopes that I wouldn't release the contents of my bowels in my trousers. Half the time I would make it; the other half, I didn't. I went through countless boxers and sheets that year, constantly trying to hide my shame from my roommates.

I hear some complain about having diarrhea for a week or the fact that they haven't had a good night's sleep in awhile. I answer in my mind, "Oh yeah, try never ever having a solid bowel movement for five years straight and not remembering when you hadn't woken up in the middle of the night to make a dead sprint to the toilet." I held to that mindset for a while. I was the victim. Things were happening to me that were beyond my control, and no one, or so I thought, was dealing with the pain that I felt day in and day out.

This wasn't the case, but in my naïve worldview, I saw the happenings of life in a biased way. My presuppositions gave me compassion for others who were hurting, but not to those who "weren't hurting enough." I shake my head in disgust as I write these words now, for I was so warped in my thinking. I know now that we all go through our own personal hell at times. It may range from emotional pain to physical pain, but who am I to say that one pain is worse than the other? How we deal with this pain is another story. A blown knee to a professional athlete can be just as devastating as a liver transplant was to me. The world may not deem it so, but God knows our thoughts and knows that we both deal with the same parkins //

mental struggle. Does He not care more about our hearts and intentions, rather than our actions?

The medications that drugged my entire system affected me in
such a way that I would get pounding headaches as well. I can remember clearly one afternoon when this happened, and I contacted
my nurse coordinator in hopes of a remedy. After all, did I need to
deal with cluster headaches as well as the headaches that are deemed
worse in pain than regular migraines?

She told me nonchalantly that there might be flare-ups in this
new area of pain because of the large doses of steroids that I was
taking, and that I couldn't really do anything about it. So every time
that I felt the beginnings of a pounding sensation, I would instinc-
tively run to my cabinet of medicine and down Vicodin as soon as
possible in hopes of drowning the pain. Much to my dismay, rarely
would I catch it in time, and I would have to miss class because of fits
of vomiting in my room.

One afternoon in particular, I remember laying in my room with
the shades drawn, both roommates away at class, and looking up at
the ceiling. Daydreams were a common experience for me, something that I ran to when I had to deal with so much pain. With the
trash can close at hand, my thoughts drifted off.

DAYDREAM

*I was running, running away from something or running to some-
thing. The ground was carpeted with a thick green grass and God's
breath was whisking away the hair from my face. Clouds could be seen
in the distance over a small patch of trees, and the sun was shining
in full view, striking my pale skin, giving way to the beginnings of a
sunburn. Stopping, I turned around, and what I saw before me was
my castle. A once-glorious structure reduced to ruins and crumbling
before my very eyes, the castle's stones were hurling themselves at me.
No matter how hard I tried, I couldn't escape the arch of the stones. My*

small strides took me inches away from each brick, dodging them as I grasped for life.

Piece by piece, my ruined heap fell closer to the ground as each rock fiber grew together, lurched off of the ground, and hurled its body towards mine. Why was it doing this? Was there something magical about this structure?

No, nothing magical, and in truth, something very plain. Up in front of me lay a vast ocean bluer than anything I had ever seen before, giving Solomon a run for his sapphires. Looking up above my tattered head, I saw clouds formed mockingly to spite me.

Almost out of reach of the strong arc of fire from the castle's stones, I neared the ocean's security. Wanting to dive in right away, both arms outstretched, I jumped headfirst into what I thought was a deep pool. Of course, with my luck, it was not the case, and I broke my nose on the tough ocean floor just inches below the surface of blue. It was not a deep ocean floor, only inches deep, mocking my hope. Lying there on the ground in what was no deeper than a puddle, I turned my body around. As the blood poured forth from my nose onto my chest, I stayed there, on my back, beckoning the stones to come. And they did. This was my life, and pain always found me.

CONTINUED DREAM

Waking up from that dream, with my salty sweat drenching me from head to toe, I reached over for the trash can and directed the lack of contents in my stomach to an already full trash can. Looking up at my ceiling once again, my eyes lost themselves in the darkness, and I faded off to sleep once more. I was quickly becoming tired from all of the pain. I wanted no more, and in my anguished cries to God, I pleaded my case before his throne, the throne that seemed empty and without a care. In my confusion and exhausted anger, I tucked away those feelings, knowing that a "good little Christian" didn't have those thoughts.

My freshmen year in college continued as such, fighting the pain from my bowels each night, dealing with the effects of the medication that turned the gray matter in my head to liquid Jell-O, and trying to find the bathroom wherever I went. During that trying time, I also met the most beautiful woman in the world who had the most infectious smile. She was so shy, so sweet, and so compassionate. Her name was Kelly, and after we went out on one date, we never stopped. Dates with her consisted of a nice dinner that included two or three visits to the bathroom and at least one or two pit stops while driving in my car. I could never enjoy a full movie with her, and I was constantly seeking out the blue triangular sign that proclaimed "men's bathroom." The upside to that is that I have probably seen more architectural designs to bathrooms than most people, and I have found a sadistic appreciation for those now beautiful constructs that were the source of my relief. It is all about the little things.

That year, the divorce of my parents was finalized, and with that finality came a certain sting that numbed even more of my molested emotions.

I was walking one evening from the cafeteria to my dorm room when my mother called me on my cell phone. In a tired and beaten voice, she related to me her concern for my well-being, and as a typical response, I expressed my cold feelings of relief that the drama of their terrible divorce was finally over. Inside, however, was an entirely different story. Images of graduations, marriages, and any holidays were marred with being torn as to with whom I would celebrate them. *What would my wedding be like? Was it going to be awkward my entire life, or would God use time as the healing factor as He has done in so many other's lives?*

I thought back on the happy times, when I was naïve and used to ask my dad to play catch with a baseball, learning to throw curves to the invisible San Francisco Giants because I was the star Dodger pitcher. They were times when the grass in our backyard became the stage to which I fought all of my army battles, and the only concern was when dinner was served. I had memories of holidays spent in the most beautiful of living rooms and remember the feel of expectations as we would scour the house in hopes of finding that hidden

Easter basket. Those memories I will cherish and store away, thinking back when life seemed more simple; never to be actualized except in the reoccurrences of my mind. They will always be precious to me.

There is a photograph that I treasure in safekeeping within the memoirs of my mind, kept safe in the storehouses of a freedom that wasn't dirtied with the corrupt anger and destruction of divorce. In the picture, the sun was out in full glory, shining through the tree that stood as a gate to our old house, a gate that protected and pleased the eye. It provided a much-needed shade amidst the heat that comes with Easter time. Around '85 or '86, our clothes marked the decadence of a decade that sought pastels and light colors, following the trend into which most would eventually fall. Our family was no exception, and in that bright morning hue, we held each other as a loving family. My father and mother held one another in what seemed like a lost desire, with smiles exuding a happiness of contentment. Their bodies were close, clinging on to something that at that time had already begun to fade. My oldest brother, swept up in the eighties and a southern California surfing mentality, stood as a pillar on the side of my beautifully dressed mother. With a football player's body, he showed a cocky smile and a confidence of one who could win over any girl in his path. He was solid.

Josh, the middle brother of three, stood next to my dad with a sheepish grin. Knowing him, he no doubt had in mind a trick up his sleeve that he lacked the muster to actually perform.

Such a young time filled with naïveté and the innocence that would soon be corrupted by extreme trials.

We had the *Beaver Cleaver* family, with the perfect house and the perfect car. Our perfection was personified, like the model family that we desperately tried to portray, through the debonair good looks of my father, the gorgeous face of my mother, and the handsome looks passed down to their three boys. Everything was as it was supposed to be, and wearing a smile that I now long to have, I stood to the left of my brother, holding the perfect family dog. My short spiked hair stood on end, and I knew no pain. No pain! Such a thought transcends all comprehension, knowing that the lost art of that innocuous thinking can never be attained again.

That picture represents to me a time when happiness was at its apex, and not for financial stability. Riches mean nothing to me now, and I see that, for no amount of property or material gifts can bring me back that family of which I was once a part. That happiness was present because of a security that I felt. I knew my father loved me. I knew that my mother loved me. I knew through the constant bruises on my arms and legs that my brothers loved me, too (they expressed it through their fists at an incredible rate). But somehow, through the sun and amidst the pastel clothes, I knew love that surpassed all, and I knew family. I knew love. I had peace.

LEARNING

"Don't be deceived, my dear brothers. Every good and perfect gift is from above, coming down from the Father of the heavenly lights, who does not change like shifting shadows. He chose to give us birth through the word of truth, that we might be a kind of firstfruits of all He created." (James 1.16,17)

"Which of you, if his son asks for bread, will give him a stone? Or if he asks for a fish, will give him a snake? If you, then, though you are evil, know how to give good gifts to your children, how much more will your Father in heaven give good gifts to those who ask Him!" (Matthew 7.9–11)

The love of God is something so transcendent over our lives that it perplexes us to our very cores. *If these trials are happening to me, if these headaches and constant bowel movements filled with blood are truly happening to me, and if God is indeed in control of everything, then why does He allow it to happen?* Most Christians believe that God blesses us, and his blessings are easily seen throughout our day. The gift of life, the breath we breathe through our lungs and the thousands of sinews, muscles and bones that must move perfectly so that we can give hugs are all taken for granted. We are a generation that focuses on pain, on the hurt and confusion that consumes our day.

When we talk about our days with loved ones or friends, do we not automatically jump to the bad things that happen to us? Some will say "no," that they focus on the good in life and not the bad. Do I have such a poor outlook on my generation as to paint this awful picture of pessimism over it, or do I have examples that will make my defense seem strong? Listen to me, if we have ten things that happen to us that are blessings but one act that penetrates our minds with stress or discomfort, are we not quick to respond by sharing that circumstance to the nearest passerby?

At best, if we get into conversations with our friends about our days, and nothing too terribly exciting happened, we speak without emotions, with based and lowly feelings explained throughout the existence of that day. We do this, of course, only if nothing bad happens or nothing incredibly awesome that excites us. Here is an example of a make-believe day: *"Honey, I had four meetings today, had lunch with a friend who told me a joke that I can't seem to re-member right now, answered a few phone calls at my desk and had to fix the fax machine in order to get the purchase orders necessary for an upcoming event."*

Blah, but throughout this make-believe day, did I focus any at-tention on the *huge* blessings that are hidden between the lines? Wonderful blessings like the job I was currently employed in, a job that I didn't deserve in the first place? No, I didn't mention either of these blessings.

"But wait," you may say. "You are educated, and you went to school so you could get a job like that in the first place. Why wouldn't you deserve the job?"

The current mindset that we all fall into at most times is this: We have worked hard in life and deserve the things given to us. The small blessings throughout our day are not truly seen as blessings; they are seen as rights to which we believe we are entitled.

I realize that I have gone off on a tangent, but I believe it is perti-nent to the issue at hand. When I had those headaches, when I visited the bathroom those countless times in the terribly dark hours of the night, when my walking towards the bathroom was interrupted by foreign pains unknown to my abdomen that made me feel as if the entire world was cramping and rolling in my intestines, I found that God's love was still wonderful to me.

How can I say that?

Instead of constantly focusing on the horrific trials that besieged my puny body, I found solace in a God that always welcomed me into His arms. I can understand getting extremely angry at God if I had no blessings, but this was not the case for me. The air I breathe in my healthy lungs *alone* is enough to feel blessed. Make no mistake; it is enough for any of us to feel blessed.

But I didn't live a perfect life, nor was I perfect in any way. What was I indeed blessed with? I could write novels on that alone, but some small, meager examples of the volumes of blessings I had each day could be summed up in the fact that I was indeed living. I was walking, breathing, loving, studying, thinking cognitively, laughing, crying, dreaming, hoping, caring, seeing beauty around every corner, surfing, swimming, camping, driving, running, reading, playing, falling and rising, smiling, hugging, talking, just to name a few. In effect, I was living, and living well by all standards. I had a roof over my head, I had meals that I had access to three times a day, and I had a wonderful family and a wonderful girlfriend that loved me more than anything.

What are your blessings that you take for granted every day and hardly raise a voice to mention in your conversations with others? I say hallelujah to those blessings! If you are reading this, you are alive! We need to wake up from the dream that plagues the world today, the dream that screams that we deserve a life we see on the television and movie screens. We are so blessed, but we are so quick to forget about the good things because those are not often the most easily seen. We are a culture bent on seeking a grass that is greener than our own, always looking out instead of looking in to find a heart so blessed. But the greatest blessing of all is something so incredibly amazing I could hardly do justice in describing.

Romans 3.23 says that, *"all have sinned and fall short of the glory of God,"* and most end that quote with just that, falling short. However, the very next verse tells of our wondrous blessing better than anything I could say: *" . . . and are justified freely by His grace through the redemption that came by Christ Jesus."* It is faith in God, and not something we come up with or conjure by our own strength, that saves us. Is there anything greater than that? If I could concentrate on any one thing in life as I go about my pathetic day living for myself, it would be focusing on my sweet Jesus and what He did for me on that cross. Did I deserve that? By no means, but nonetheless, the power of what was accomplished is freely given to me. And it is that merciful and glorious act that gets me through even the most incredible of trials.

We have a tendency to look at what is wrong with our lives, comparing them to others and what we "feel" is appropriate and "right." We look at God and have this evil outlook towards Him, shoving Him in a box that He doesn't deserve to be in because of how we view our biographies. We see our lives and our trials and immediately turn to God for an answer, for a defense as to His actions. How sad that we cannot see what He truly blesses us with every single day. How terribly pathetic that we cannot wake up from the dreams that have so trapped us into the mode of thinking we are in. We often fail to see the Lord of Creation and His beautiful gifts lavished on us so much more abundantly than anything we could possibly imagine. How terribly sad indeed, for God's love is clearly seen once we wake up from our daydreams.

anger

tired but anxious, I stepped with regard into my new apartment. After hauling my wares to San Diego from my house in Palos Verdes, my thoughts were guarded. What was this year going to be like as I stepped into a new time? Were the rubber bands of trials going to pull me back, challenging me once again, or was I finally free from the worry that had come to form the very sinew that made my heart? Was this year going to be different than so many previously? Dear Lord, I pray that it is so.

Jeff Block and Sam Kobeilush, two great friends, were projected to be my roommates who were going to share my heart, my worries, and my joy that year. Knowing full well my history, they still took the chance of having me help carry the burden of payment that a condo in Ocean Beach inevitably would bring. And that condo was something else. Let me say that it was my first condo; so hopefully, you're conjuring up images in your own mind of your first rental when away at college for the first time. I laugh now, but it was a palace to me, even though a putrid smell of burnt fish wafted through our senses from every area of the carpet. The carpet color itself was a dusty blue, dusty because of the stains that the previous tenant so graciously left behind. The condo consisted of two bedrooms, two bathrooms, and a square foot of space that was labeled a kitchen. In all actuality, the place wasn't that bad. We were only one block from the beach and less than five minutes away from our college turned university.

I remember the first night that we stayed together as a roommate faction, for how could you forget something like that? The neighbors were having a battle as to who could be the loudest, and even though it was a weeknight, they were having a party or something. In fact, we later learned that it would be rare if we didn't have something going on in our complex. If the radios weren't blaring their music all night, we would be woken up by a random flyby that reminded us of the movie "Top Gun." Situated just south of the international airport, we were fortunate enough to hear the soft lull of 747s scream overhead, coupled with the noises of our alcoholic next door neighbor. Boy, was he ever a joy! I loved coming home late at night scared out of my mind for fear that "Tommy" was on a rampage. Those were the days.

School started after that first weekend, and I was able to attend all of my classes on time, which, for me, was huge. I didn't have to go to the hospital that year, for my liver disease was somewhat in check, and my body was healthier because of all the surfing that I was doing. I was on the planning committee for events at Point Loma, so I remained very active with activities and sports games. The biggest games to go to, since we didn't have a football team, were the basketball and soccer games; they usually involved more yelling and making each other laugh because of our antics than actually watching the games. Kelly and I were dating still, but only God knows why she was still with me, and we continued our incredible regime of going out two to three times a week. Little did my dad know that most of his support that he gave me monthly went to that investment, though I am quite sure he will not be angry with that decision.

On one date in particular, all of my anxieties came to a fountainhead and exploded in my face. No matter how hard I tried to live a normal life, the Lord felt it necessary to allow me to go through some exponentially harder trials that year, trials that were used to humble me in incredible ways. As usual, we were out to dinner at a restaurant called *Benihana's* and had ordered our normal *hibachi chicken*. Going to the bathroom two times in the course of an hour frustrated me, but it became such a way of life for me that I didn't really think too much on it. Kelly never said a word and always gave me the biggest smile whenever I came back from the restroom. Holding hands, we exited the table and made our way out to the 1986 Toyota Forerunner that I called my own. We made our way to downtown San Diego, strolling through random stores where we dreamed of buying furniture for our imaginary house that was more beautiful than anything we will probably ever own. As the night drew on, and as I frequented many bathrooms along the way, my body was quickly becoming exhausted from the amount of liquids I was losing, and I knew that I had to call it a night.

Most nights, before I would drop her off at her dorms, we would spend more than a few minutes enjoying each other's company, stealing long kisses that may not have been the best idea for a young man of twenty years old. Most of those kisses would have to be cut short however, because my stomach would attack me with the ongoing war I had come to expect. I found myself growing numb to the repetition of pain over and over again. And this particular night, the war raged severely without mercy. Can you imagine what it is like to actually hate your body, feeling as if the faulty shell you received at birth somehow needed a trade in, like a "lemon" car that wastes all your money on repairs that never seemed to work? I had fought the battle that was inside me many times before, but this particular night, the skirmish was more than I could handle, and I lost.

Too ashamed to go to the bathroom in the waiting area of her dorm hall, I fibbed a little and said that the pain I was feeling in my stomach and the loud noises of gas moving through my large intestine were of no concern and that I could wait to use the bathroom until I got home. The pain had become a characteristic to me, and in previous chapters, I likened the pain to an animal running around in my large intestine with a spiked helmet on. Maybe it was because the disease had grown more mature, or maybe because my body was just feeling it more, but the pain that night was even more intense than described in earlier chapters. When gas would move from one side to another, my lining would literally rip and bleed, producing a torturous biting pain that consumed all of my energy and concentration. I literally had to concentrate on not releasing my bowels in my pants, getting accustomed to holding inside that which anguished me. It was like a grenade going off in my stomach area.

I drove home, listening to the cool breeze of the ocean through my window while trying to stay cold and uncomfortable, fighting with all of my energy not to release my bowels, and driving on instinct so as not to get into a head-on accident on Sunset Cliffs Blvd. This experience was so common to me, for often times I would have to stop the car and run outside—quickly undoing my belt in hopes that I wouldn't defecate in my pants—and go to the bathroom right there in broad daylight.

I remember I had to do just that one time driving home from college on the freeway. That day was beautiful, if I remember correctly, and I could see the vast blueness of the ocean with the sun coming down ever so slightly to enhance the waves with shadows. I found myself speeding on Interstate 5 during the interim section between Oceanside and Dana Point. I prayed that I could hold the pain in my stomach until I reached the safety of the next gas station, but it consumed me so much that I had to rush to the side of the road on the busy freeway, drop my pants, and go with no concern about my lack of privacy. That turned into such a humbling experience, for I had some friends who, unbeknownst to me, were traveling right behind me. They stopped their vehicle on the side of the road with me, right as I was running behind my car to release my bowels. They got out of their car, rushed to my side to see if everything was alright, and waited for my reaction. They had no idea what was going on, so I urged them to continue to their destination. The brief pause I took to tell them to move on proved to be too much for me, and I again defecated in my pants. Fortunately, I was able to clean the mess up as well as I could, but I had to tell my girlfriend that I couldn't see her right away, for I needed to go home and change. *Why would she want to be with someone who didn't even have control of his bowels?*

Coming home from the night of my date on Sunset Cliffs with my windows rolled down was like that. I knew that I had just enough time to get home, if I didn't hit any traffic signals, to make it to the toilet. So I was holding the waste matter in my intestine as long and as hard as I could, praying that this wouldn't be another night where I got humbled. Each passing intersection was like a game of chance; sometimes I even went through red lights and prayed that no police officers were going to pull me over. What would they think if I rushed out of my car in a sprint as they pulled me over? Would they in turn not freak out as I dropped my pants in front of them?

Then it happened, I hit my first signal, just a few miles from home. The pain was insurmountable as I did everything I could to keep the inevitable wastes from being released too soon. *Oh, Lord, give me the strength to make it to the toilet, please. I beg you.*

The music in my car was off, for I had to concentrate with everything in me; I wanted no distractions. It was like a battle with my body, not knowing if I was going to lose but knowing that I had very little chance to win. The last left turn came as I made it to the parking spot in the alley behind my apartment. I couldn't move however, as the sudden change in position would surely generate enough momentum to trigger the release, so I carefully planned out my escape. The hurt came in spurts, like birth pains, so I had to ride out this last attack before I made my move.

So close to the toilet now, just feet away from my door, I put the car in park and opened my door. The feeling of a thousand elephants running around in my body overcame me. The feces came out little by little as my muscles became raw from the pain. *Not now God, I have made it this far, please not now . . . I am pleading with You.*

I knew the enemy had just fired a canon, scoring a direct hit as I couldn't hold it anymore. As I jumped out of my car, praying that not too much would slip out, I could feel the warmth of my stools slowly fill my pants. Each step I took released the pressure that had built up so potently in my body, releasing more and more as I got closer and

daydreams // an end to my nightmares

daniel parkins //

closer. As I reached for the screen door to my apartment, I danced in place to find the correct key in order to unlock what became to me a wall; I stepped into my comfort zone and rushed to the bathroom. *Please Lord, let there be no one using my bathroom right now.* A few feet away from the toilet, I felt the trickle of waste run down my leg and into my shoe and onto the floor, like little rabbit pellets marking my territory. I dropped my pants that were covered in sludge on the inside and released the pressure that became my humbling instrument. After I finished, I turned on the shower and stepped into the warmth with all of my clothes on. In tears, I sank down in the tub with the water rushing over me.

Why was this happening to me? What did I do?

Those were the thoughts that consumed my thinking as I did my best to clean my clothes. I drifted off into the private world of escape that took residency in my mind again, absolutely exhausted as I felt the water massage my scalp.

DAYDREAM

My leg was bandaged up, and I found myself sitting in the middle of a large oasis. The palm trees were flowing in the wind, the birds in the air circling me with a mesmerized screech from above. I didn't know what I was doing there, but I knew that I had just come from a battle of sorts that had just taken place over the horizon. All alone in the middle of the desert, I curled up in a ball to die, praying that the Lord would take me quick.

A thought came to me . . . what Lord? This isn't a battle? What was this sick game I was playing where all of the rules that I knew by heart were broken and nothing seemed to make sense. This isn't fair. Games are supposed to be fair.

That's it! It wasn't a battle that I just fought; it was a game I had just lost. But what was the difference? They had become one and the same to me there as I lay with the sand as my bed.

I looked up at the sky and saw the laughing sun attempting to break apart my skin with its hurtful rays, coupled with the birds of death circling overhead as its partner in my doom.

Just then, I heard a noise, and what was before me was the tail of a scorpion in full view. It looked to be five feet across, for that was how close it was to my nose. With steadiness, I got up slowly and fumbled for my shoe. With moments, if not seconds, to spare, I unlaced the leather around my foot and took a swing at my new enemy, hoping to dash the little bit of life to which it clung.

A direct hit scored the death and enabled me to make another notch on my belt, yet one blow was not enough to satisfy me. I continued to strike the scorpion multiple times, just as Mel Gibson's character in The Patriot lunged time after time with his weapon on the already dead soldier. Where was I? I looked around for a few minutes to survey the landscape and realized that I was still banging the sand with a sadistic gaze in my eyes. I wanted to find anything to hit, to destroy.

Laying still for over an hour lured the idiotic birds into direct contact with me. They began nibbling at my toes, drawing blood as I fooled them into thinking that I was a dead man. Wasn't I?

Just as a vulture started picking at my hand, I grabbed its beak and sent the other birds flying. Twisting the beak in my hands, I squeezed the life out of the bird, drawing blood out of its broken mouth. Using my hands, I pummeled the feathered creature in its lifeless body, ripping its glory out one shred at a time. Anger flooded my senses, and for all intents and purposes, I saw red and desired vengeance. Death was not enough for this creature as I grabbed sand and shoved it down its body. Taking it by its neck, I flung it from side to side, shaking the very ground that I was laying on, feathers flying everywhere. Somehow, through my rage, tears came, and I started bawling. This was not enough. This was not filling the emptiness that I was feeling inside. I was so alone, and killing this bird did nothing for me. Rage consumed me, and I searched around for something, anything, to get my attention off of the heinous crime that I had just committed. I tried walking to the water that the oasis held, but my leg was injured, so I just crawled.

CONTINUED DREAM

I recovered from the bowel incident the very next day, pushing it out of my mind as I headed off to school. I was now clean, the sheets in my bed were clean, and I was wearing clean clothes. That day, I went to the bathroom over twenty times, and often those bowel movements were filled with blood. I knew that I couldn't live like this, and a conversation I had previously with my father told me that I had the option to have surgery on my large intestine. It basically meant that I would have my entire large intestine removed with promises that I wasn't going to have to deal with this pain anymore. That was a promise that I held on to, a promise that I couldn't let go of, a promise to me that offered hope and a freedom from what consumed every part of me. It was a hope in a dream.

I dropped out of school in October to get my entire large intestine removed, and had all of the funding from that semester returned, which was a blessing for my father. My disease had taken control of my life, literally dictating where I was going. Whenever going any-where I would always have to know where the closest bathrooms were located, just in case an emergency happened. I started carrying around tissue wherever I went, and baby wipes took up permanent residence in my mode of transportation.

When I finally came home, after realizing my dire need of the removal of my entire large intestine, we called the doctors, and they told me that surgery wouldn't be possible until late January. All I wanted to do was finish school, so this was another blow I had to deal with.

Struggling to find sanity, I remember one evening curling up in a ball in my room and my mother coming in. The finalization of the divorce was still fresh in her mind, and to see her son having to go through another major surgery all over again was difficult to bear. For me, it was heartbreaking.

She took me by the hand and raised me to my knees and just stroked my head as I lay in her arms, consumed with pain and tears.

The floodgates opened wide that day, and my anger got the best of me. *Why did I have to go through this? Why?* As I bawled in her arms, we reached the end of our ropes, and God's gift of faith was the only thing, and I mean the only thing, that got us through. The sheer number of trials at my relatively young age was a weight on my back that broke me, and in that instant, I lost hope. I was praying fervently that God would take me home, if there still was a God, though deep down inside I knew that there was.

Many people tried telling me that this pain and these trials were for my own good, that they were molding me into the "man" God wanted me to be. Was I supposed to be stronger because of this, or did that theology mean that God, in His sovereignty, planned beforehand the torment I had to face daily? I went to the bathroom twenty times a day, with my stools often filled with blood, and I was supposed to be thankful? Are you kidding me? What kind of a God would allow that? These were the questions I was struggling with during that semester I had to drop out of the university; these were the questions that plagued me when I closed my eyes to sleep—a sleep that never was sound, nor one that ever made it through the entire night.

That time was also filled with grief in other areas, for I had just been put on an experimental medication for my liver that supposedly enhanced and helped out the situation with my large intestine. Supposedly, it was an anti-inflammatory medication coupled with an antirejection agent and an immunosuppressive characteristic. I say *supposedly*, for I will never know. The first time taking the medication served to be a disaster for my weakened body, and to this day I still have horror-filled dreams about it.

The nurse coordinator called the night I picked up the medication, and through a sketchy message that was replayed many times, we heard that I was supposed to take five CC's of the stuff. So without hesitation, I downed the diluted medication in orange juice and waited for my next dosage. Two dosages later, my mother called the nurse coordinator just to be sure that I was taking the proper amount, and it turns out that I needed to take five tenths of a CC. In other words, I took so much of the medication that my body reacted violently, and I was not only depleted of energy, but of my self worth as well. By the time I stopped taking that wretched medication, I had thirty-four canker sores on my tongue, in my throat, and all around the lining of my mouth. I developed boils on my neck and back that turned into mountainous sores, growing from deep within my body. It hurt to even talk, the pain being excruciating, and it was hard for me to leave the house for the stark humiliation factor.

And the boils didn't go away for quite some time. A month later, my hair was so shaggy that I had to get a haircut, so I made my appointment accordingly. Most of the sores had left and worked their way out to the surface of my skin and healed, but one in particular ravaged me. It was located right in the middle of the back of my neck, and I had to go to the barber with regret and a forced humility. Sitting in the chair left me ashamed, for the giant sore was protruding vividly, and I could tell he was grossed-out by it. He didn't know what to do with it, so he didn't trim the hair at the very bottom of my hair line, and I left there with a quiet reserve, humbled to my core. I had become disgusting.

Weeks after that, it was even larger than it had been when I visited the barber, and I knew I had to do something about it. I went to the skin doctor, and after the shock on his face wore off, he took his scalpel and punctured the sore. A bright green puss trickled down my back before he could get enough gauze to stop it, and it was the grossest experience I have ever had. My heart went out to Job, who was covered in those things, and my identification with that Bible character grew stronger and stronger.

Knowing that I couldn't miss another semester of school, I went back to college without having the surgery, which proved to be a mistake. Every night I would wake up two to three times and run to the toilet in hopes that I would not release my bowels in my boxers. Often times I would stumble in my sleepiness and fail in my endeavor. But that wasn't the hardest thing that I had to deal with that semester, though it was related to that despicable disease.

One night—right before I went to sleep, as my ritual of going to the bathroom would inevitably time itself—when I lifted up from the toilet, what lay before my eyes caused a sense of sheer horror. Excuse me for being graphic, but I want you to understand what I saw. Chunks of blood lay in the toilet, with nothing brown, only red. It was so filled with blood that I couldn't see the bottom of the toilet, and I melted.

Shocked, then turning suddenly calm, I went to my roommate without flushing the toilet. Daniel Hunt was the poor soul that witnessed a glimpse of what I saw almost every day, and he turned white. Up to that point, I had never asked anyone to see nor look at my feces, but I had to have a witness of what just happened. He didn't say a word, and I don't presume to know what he was thinking, but the look on his face said enough. Right away, I called my girlfriend, waking her up, and told her that my large intestine had just exploded, that the lining broke, and that I wasn't going to make it through the night.

Could you imagine hearing those words from a boyfriend that you were deeply in love with? What would you do? Maybe it has happened to you, where you have heard terrible news such as that, but waking up to those words was an incredible thing for Kelly. As we ended the call, she demanded that I tell her that I was going to be okay, and with that, I laid down on my bed for what I presumed to be my last night's sleep. Some would ask, "Why didn't you go to the Emergency Room?" The truth is I welcomed the idea of going home to be with God, for I was tired with my life.

I wasn't worried, and I think I know why. God had been doing a major work in my life and had shown me through others and through his Word that I had a different calling in life, one that was exponentially harder than most. But almost every day, I prayed that God would either take away the pain or send me to my real home. I longed to be in the Father's arms, for who wouldn't? To not have to deal with the pain I faced daily would be sheer elation. So I closed my eyes, praying that God would take me in my sleep, and have never slept better since.

exhausted

fter that dreadful and intensely personal night in the dorms, I awoke to a new day and a new lease on life. I hadn't died that evening, and as the sun rose with the new morning, so my hope increased and began to show. I hadn't yet been defeated. The rest of that semester, I battled fervently for my life and for my sanity, trying to deal with the constant affects of my large intestine disease. It was difficult to say the least, and I barely made it through.

May of '99 ended with me in the hospital again, but this time it was because of the pneumonia that had racked my body. I had contracted this virus up in Mammoth during my mother's wedding. That was such a wonderful time—the wedding that is—but the pneumonia racked my body. I wasn't able to finish my finals, so the classes were never credited to me. Another wasted semester left me sprawling for ideas as to how I was ever going to get my bachelor's degree in Theology/Philosophy. The man my mother married is one of the most godly men I have ever met and still continues to love me unconditionally. Though advanced in years, he is a man who has a child's heart changed by the Molder of clay Himself; a heart that, when seen through a smile, can fill a room with both compassion and laughter. I am blessed to call him my step-father and am forever changed because of his open arms.My own father and I had had a sketchy relationship from the effects of the divorce that needed some serious mending. I "secretly" held an incredible bitterness whenever I was around him and let him into my life as little as possible. I know that he knew this, and I know that it was wearing on him, also. So my dad planned a trip for us, scheduled right before I was going to have all six feet of my large intestine removed. He wanted me to go with him to London and Paris, and with that enticing notion of adventure, we set out early that summer. Little did I know that it would be one of the most important trips of my life, for my father loved me despite my bitterness, and he knew exactly what I needed.

The trip itself was amazing, and as we touched down in Heathrow Airport, we embarked on a grand adventure. We were no longer father and son, so to speak, for we quickly became friends of the highest caliber. My dad is a man's man, one with a wit more intelligent than most, and one that can make anyone feel welcomed with laughter. I was a scrawny kid who probably thought too highly of himself, but he was the kind of father who always made me feel so good-looking. He helped me forget about my downfalls with disease and struggle, and never said a word whenever I needed to visit the toilet. He would always point out the girls who would be looking at me and was always proud of his son. He made me feel special when I didn't feel like it and always got my mind off of the pain.

London proved to be spectacular; we moved freely from one part of the city to another on the Underground, and it was the friendliest place I have ever visited. The people there made me feel warm and welcomed, and since that trip I have wanted to move there. Each night, my father and I would spend a couple of hours sitting outside the famous pub where Jack the Ripper supposedly ate. "Gee," you are probably thinking, "That's great, what a wonderful place to have a couple of Cider beers." Well, the truth is, I felt akin to Jack, for I had my insides ripped out and was going to have some more surgery done to me. Though that sick man was no doubt deranged in an incredible way, I laughed inside to think of the horror he would have felt if he started in on me. Is that sick? I probably shouldn't have said that, but nonetheless, I am going for honesty in this treatise I am writing.

One memory I will tell you about, before I bore you to death with my mental photo album, was when we first reached Paris by the underground train from London. My father and I, in a word, were lost. He and I laugh about it now, and I think we laughed about it then, but we didn't know a lick of the French language and didn't know how to get to our hotel room. We must have walked five miles in a building not much bigger than a large church, wandering from platform to platform, trying to piece together some sort of direction. We must have looked completely lost, for that is what we were, but hauling around that luggage was a sight I wish we could have filmed.

Finally reaching our hotel, the Californian of all places, we ventured out into another great unknown. Walking along one of the major streets in Paris, we became insatiably hungry and were anxious to find some food. The first café we found suited us perfectly, and we collapsed on an outside table. Lo and behold, my father strikes up a conversation with an older woman, just to "mingle with the laid-back country folk." She hears our English and starts inquiring if we are knowledgeable in any other languages found around Paris, such as French, German, Italian, and the like. My father continued to insist that we only knew English, though she didn't seem satisfied with our answer. She then asked where we lived in England, and we told her that we were Americans. With that, she stood up, made a spit gesture to the ground, and walked off, yelling at us.

What? My father and I were flabbergasted.

We looked around for support in hopes of finding an explanation. One man holding a newspaper and smoking a cigarette—for they all smoked cigarettes over there—told us in broken English and French that she was probably pregnant. We both laughed at that, but I didn't understand this. Why was my father laughing? The nice French man told the other people in the café his joke in his native language, and a raucous laughter ensued. My dad leaned over to explain to me, "I think he was trying to say that it was her 'time of the month.'" Of course I became offended right away and wanted to stand up for all women in regards to that comment . . . but truth be known, I thought it was hilarious. And if Kelly reads this, I might be going to heaven sooner than I thought.

On the flip side, we enjoyed Paris but spent most of the time recovering from jet lag. In doing that, we watched a lot of the French Open on T.V. and were fortunate enough to see and meet a few of the tennis stars who were staying at our hotel. It was such a special experience and such a bonding time with my father that it left an indelible mark on my psyche. That trip finally put a bandage on the wound I felt my father inflicted with the divorce, and slowly, my bitterness began to heal. A few years later, after many yelling matches and misunderstandings, I was finally able to forgive him.

Coming back to the states was such a blessing. People who spoke English were never taken for granted again. I can't imagine the frustration of God's people when He scattered them by creating different languages because they were trying to build a tower up to heaven. We didn't care if the people were mean or if they were nice, and I think it was the calmest I have ever seen my dad drive in traffic. People were actually driving on the correct side of the road. But I was sure elated when I reached my room and took off my shoes to go to sleep. It was a trip I will never forget, for it was a trip shared by two estranged friends who regained their friendship.

A few weeks later, my large intestine, my bane, my humiliating disease, was cut from my body, and surgery destroyed me once more.

After the surgery removed my entire large intestine, I remember lying in the hospital bed, having woken up from what seemed to be a nightmare. Turning my head to one side, my clouded vision cleared its haze and focused on my mother. She was sitting there, all quiet with her legs crossed, reading her devotionals, no doubt, from Oswald Chambers' *Streams in the Desert*, or A.W. Tozer's *On the Holy Spirit*. Those are, to her, "semi-scriptures;" semi in the sense of being nowhere near infallible, yet capable of encouragement and speaking Holy-Spirit-led truths into her life. And there she was, as she could be found in any of my trials, right by my side. I know undying support from my mother, for she embodies the very definition of it.

The effects of abdominal surgery, and any surgery for that matter, are such that your digestive track, for a time, ceases to function properly. This is due to the side effects of the necessary yet toxic drugs taken prior to surgery. Coupled with "knocking you out," the drugs "put to sleep" your intestines and digestive track as well. The first thing I remember that day was an insatiable thirst and not having the ability to alleviate that plague.

The next thing I did—as I always do after every major surgery, sad as it is that I can say that—was lift up my hospital gown to survey my mutilated skin. A fresh wound stapled shut was what caught my eye. Though not startled, for I had seen this gruesome sight before, my fingers touched each staple with a wince. The familiar sensation of having no feeling in my abdomen sent me back to visions and memories of my first liver transplant a few years before, and I was haunted by the dichotomy of the two.

To the right of my own reading railroad was something so foreign to me that I didn't quite know what to do with it. Protruding from my skin right above my stomach's waistline was something I knew would be there but couldn't prepare for. The sight appalled me and sent me reeling. I was disgusted by my body once again, for what I saw was my own small intestine poking through my stomach, leading to an attached bag that collected the wastes my body produced. I couldn't take my eyes off of the anomaly for a long time, taking mental pictures of the pink blob newly formed on my skin. I couldn't help but think, as I lay there looking at it, that it was similar to the larger pink blob that had caused me so much pain for as long as I could remember. I was so glad to *finally* be rid of it.

In the sickly substance that digested my food, was there somehow an essence of freedom? Was this the twisted Wizard behind my curtain in the body that was my own Oz? Was this a joke? So much pain. So much anguish. So much hurt. So much humility breaking down so much pride. Somehow, seeing my small intestine in its full glory brought down the demonic powers of control I had once given my large intestine, and I started to laugh.

And in that laughter I found a joy I had not experienced for quite some time—the sweet joy of victory. For twenty years the civil war in my body had raged, and though the battle was far from over, my Gettysburg had finally come. For so long I had found defeat after defeat after defeat, and the enemy—the anger, frustration, pain, near depression, hurts, doubts and fears—had fought bravely and won decisive victories. Like Hannibal riding on the backs of elephants, the enemy had used brilliant strategies in its defeat of my pride and everything I held as dear.

But this was victory indeed. It was something the enemy had not expected, for who could have known a young man would readily choose to suffer to expedite the removal of future suffering? If the devil uses logic, I believed that this confused him, and in the Civil War that was my body, I sent him back to Virginia to lick his wounds. I made the conscious decision to have my entire large intestine removed, finally eliminating the long term suffering with a brief amount of pain from the surgery.

There I was, lying on the bed of pure white, stained by the fluids that were leaking out of me, staring at my symbol of freedom. Now how could I say that? I felt freedom, though tied to a bag that collected my excrements, because I was told empty promises about how this was going to be the last major hurdle that I would have to jump over. This was going to be the last battle that my body would see, or so I thought and so I was led to believe. No more pain! No more rushing to the bathroom with fear that I would defecate in my pants! No more humiliations on the side of the road! That reality had always been just a dream to me, and in my naïve hope, I strained for the future as I was lying in the bed.

I remember clearly during my two-week stay in the hospital that year, as I would inevitably dose off to sleep every night, how each day gave me more and more hope. Not hope in the real, but a hope of something not experienced, a hope in the surreal. I had been through so much pain in my life—particularly that year—that my memories were muddled with dreams and truth. Sometimes I remembered things, thinking that I did actually experience them, when in all actuality they were just dreams. I lived in dreams sometimes, and on that bed away from home, the bed I know all too well, I escaped through dreams.

I didn't want to deal with the excruciating pain of having had my intestines ripped from my now mutilated body coupled with not being able to move because of other incisions. Sometimes I would lie there in the bed, hearing screams from other patients trying to recover from surgery as well. They would pierce my ears at night, and as I was greatly affected by the medication, I would roll over on my stomach and forget about the recent surgery, trying to cover my ears. Needless to say, milliseconds later I would join the chorus of screams that would echo up and down the hall, because I would rip my incisions after each roll. My screams would fill the hospital with the shouts that only the prospect of death could bring. Those shouts became familiar to me, because the pain was nearly unbearable.

Those nights haunt me now, particularly since I am writing about it, and always send me back to a place where life was so uncertain . . . but is there really any difference now? As I write this, I sit in a room that is my home away from home, in beautiful Crowley Lake. How is this really different than the hospital bed when it comes down to it? Take away the pain, take away the suffering and machines, take away the nurses and the cold stench of cleanliness, take away the comfort of people, and I am left with myself. All we have that we can see, and this is a scary thought, is ourselves. But I can say confidently that I know Jesus, and in Him I am now alive. That was the truth I learned that time in the hospital. I was not my own. My Lord purchased me, and I had Him there beside me. He never left my side, even when I woke up in the middle of the night, my bed wet with bodily fluids.

Christ was quickly becoming the cornerstone of my faith, and in those trials I found Him. Truth be known, I think it was Jesus who revealed Himself to me, but I know that I had Him with me as I left the hospital to go home. The drive itself was no easy task as each jolt in the car, each bump on the road, was to me a hurricane of trials. By the time I made it to my father's condo, I was completely exhausted from the pain. My incision was still very sore, so I gingerly laid down in bed, on my back, and fell into a deep sleep. *Lord, let me sleep.*

DAYDREAM

Tied to a stake by my wrists, I didn't know how I got there. Up in the sky was an overcast ceiling molded in marble colors of pink and yellow hue; beautiful if not for the pain around my wrists. Drawing my attention off of my immediate concerns, my mind raced for some semblance of peace. Above me, something striking caught my attention. I saw a dove dancing in the wind with one of its companions. There above my beaten brow played before me a symphony of love, just out of reach, putting to shame the best of Beethoven's classics.

As I lost myself in what seemed to be tranquility, the drumming sensation of the waves and surf against my swollen ankles woke me from the surrealistic nightmare of which I was a part. My hands, which no longer possessed any feelings, were tied behind my back, bleeding from the coarse rope that held them. I found myself tied to a stake, without any glimmer of hope, tossed and beaten to a pulp. Neither friend nor foe could recognize me as the blood drained from my face. I was swollen and barely able to breathe, but the stake offered me a sense of security—security in the fact that I wasn't going to fall, for I felt that this piece of wood was my sanctuary deeply, rooted in the gravel of my own grave of truth.

How did I get here? My legs were blue from the lack of circulation to the important vessels of blood, for they were tied with precision, also. I hung there, awaiting my doom, as one wave came after another, crashing against my weathered body. The tide was rising quickly amidst the dance of love on high. Beautiful noises could be heard just a few feet away from my ears, and the doves themselves offered no help for my situation.

Knowing that the series of events that led me to be tied to this stake was an ordeal of its own, I now took solitude and rest in what was approaching—my death, the sweet death that had so long eluded me.

But for how long? How long had I been tied to this stake? How long since I could see my own downfall and what would become the kiss of eternity? I was so tired; I wanted no more. Ages seemed to drag on forever as the waves crashed against my near lifeless body, and I longed for release.

Tired—so tired—yet all I could do was wait. Was there something miraculous in the air, or was I just fooling myself? Could the impossible happen? Could I get out of this insane predicament? Was I not a seasoned soldier, ready to commit seppuku to maintain my honor? For so long, I had been beaten by the waves, beaten by the throes of life, and now the inevitable is prolonged?

Not remembering now the events that led up to this stake story in my life, I resolved to know of the feeling life had left on me. I ran a race that I could never win, hoping against impossible odds. I was beaten, and I wanted to go home—home to the eternal; home to peace and no more pain.

It was a wish that never came true, for after my anger subsided, I found myself looking up at the sky, eyes chasing the birds to their new destination, and then looking back at the now broken piece of wood that was my security. The ropes had been chewed off, and somehow I had been freed.

God, no, please, release me. Those were the thoughts that went through my head as I sank down into the depths of the ocean, exhaling as much life as possible. Death was upon me now, for that was what I greatly desired, knowing that I couldn't take my life on my own accord. Just then, with oxygen deficiency blackening my vision, the tide pulled back and I was on the sandy shores of my life again. Breathing air sweeter than honey, drinking it down to my toes, I looked up and saw the sun beaming down on me.

I felt the warmth powerfully overtake me, closing my eyes to the penetrating glare of the center of life. Without the sun, I was hopeless, but hope found itself in the sun. The doves were back, dancing their jig to the sound of an inaudible chorus, with strands of rope in their mouths, looking for a place to start their nest. Looking for a place to start anew.

The sound of silence woke me up a few hours later, as I was not used to life without noise, and somehow, I felt refreshed. I made my way down the stairs, taking at least five minutes of my life, and yelled as loudly for my mother as I could without using stomach muscles. She was staying at my father's house, since he was out on vacation or something, and I needed someone to take care of me. That experience alone had to be a little awkward for her, but she still patiently stayed by my side. Again, my angel.

She wasn't home, hopefully taking my advice to go out and get her head clear from the stress of caring for me, so I walked outside for the first time in a couple of weeks. The sun was shining, and the breeze felt good against my skin. My father and I stayed at a beach house that he purchased after the divorce, and as I walked along the steps, making my way to the ocean, I felt alive again for the umpteenth time. I remember walking along the beach, though not very far since my energy level was close to nil, feeling the coarse sand of Redondo Beach rubbing the bottom of my feet raw. It felt great, and in that instant, with the sun breaking through the clouds and the pounding surf against my ears, I enjoyed God. Hurt, tired, confused, but secure. Security is what I felt as God's arms wrapped around me that afternoon, security in the fact that I didn't have all of the answers, but that everything was going to be okay. No clichés, no trite sayings, but security that the Creator of the universe was taking care of His very own son.

During those trials, I think I romanticized the pain of them, never dealing with the reality of it all. But what could I do? I viewed my life as different than others' lives; I was a knight on a quest to find the Holy Grail that was sorely missing in society. I lived in movies, and I lived in dreams. Each day was another chance to live in a strength not my own. With each daily pain, thoughts would drift to heroes I had immortalized in my mind, wondering what they would do. Not heroes like William Wallace or Luke Skywalker, but heroes that actually lived, such as the apostle Paul or Hudson Taylor. Heroes that shared my pain in life, shared my story somehow, and thus shared a little bit of what I was. I dreamed of myself conquering cities for Christ, as Jonah did Nineveh, and got lost in the crusades I held with Billy Graham.

My trials defined me, and in them I incorrectly found my twisted purpose and sickly meaning. They were to me my garrison that I held between the world and my superficial reality of some war epic.

I can remember clearly one time, not long after I had my large intestine removed, when I held my fists to the ground, taunting the enemy of all things holy. With the call of "Freedom!" ringing in my ears as in *Braveheart*, I echoed my own threats of puffed up pride and stupidity. *"If God calls me to it, I will go through another transplant for His name! I will not back down but will fight, and I will succeed!"* Craziness poured from my mouth that fateful October day, but I can remember the onslaught of romanticism that clouded my mind and tortured my spirit.

Not until very recently have I discovered that these trials, though haunting, do not define me. As I am no longer on that hospital bed; I am no longer a liver transplant kid. I am someone who has, no doubt, been through the fires of many surgeries; I am not made up of trials, however. Though having gone through them, I am no longer defined by them but am the better for having survived them. I cannot live in the past pain of hurt and bowel uncontrollability, but must move forward as newly burned forests must grow and resurface with life. Remaining in the past and always letting them affect me, always trudging up what happened earlier in life, is to remain the victim. Doing so is actually the antithesis of what I had romanticized in my naïve mind, for victory as the victim is impossible. We are not the trials we have gone through, nor are we controlled by them, we are only strengthened by those terrible and awesome trials.

And I had yet another defining moment, one that was promised to be the last, but in all truth turned out to be just one of many to come. All pain seems terrible at the time, and cancels out memories of other pain and heartache, for new pain seems to dull the sense on the old.

Yet this moment in time, this trial that overtook me, was pain that will transcend every fiber of my being for as long as I live. I thought I knew pain before this, but nothing compared. One always finds themselves saying with a heartfelt confidence, "This by far is the worst pain I have experienced." The truth is I have said that before in this story of my heart, yet I mean it this time. I have never experienced such a pain as that which I am about to describe.

beaten

mammoth was not my home but posed as a make-shift happiness that I was not accustomed to. After recovering from the initial shock of surgery I found myself recuperating in a home surrounded by the sweet smell of pine. Though at first the recovery process seemed to be simple, it was anything but, and my faith became not only injured, tired as well. No longer the captain of my vessel, I felt as though I was the barnacle on the back of a whale, no more than an inch in size.

I had been releasing my bowels into a bag for over three weeks now, and hate had slowly begun to claim the bitterness inside of me. Every day was marred with questions concerning the sanity of my decision to remove the entire large intestine, for the pain had not left me. In truth, it was much worse, and I was faced with the horror that I had gone through and was going through extreme pain for naught. Was it all a waste, or in time was I going to feel the healing power of modern medicine? Was it true that God's hands were with the surgeons' hands, that He indeed was in control of the situation and my life was about to change for the good?

The good? *What was that?* It had been so long since I was ten and had played in the street with my older brother outside the house. *Was it good then?* I was dealing with asthma even then and was in and out of hospitals at that young age. I don't think I had any understanding of what good could possibly mean, for trials and pain always followed me, no matter where I went, no matter how hard I tried to escape. It had been so long since I was six and the only thing I needed to worry about was obeying my mother when she called for us to come to dinner. If I were to romanticize anything in life, those times would be what I would most like to remember. A time when innocence was mine and naïveté was a blessing, when brushing your teeth seemed absurd and making your bed was a chore to end all chores. How I longed for those days, and how I dreamed of them often, hoping to escape the reality that I found myself in daily.

But was my surgery all for nothing? Was it too early to tell? If it was all for the good, then why can't I *see or feel* this good? All I saw was a bag, a prison, attached to my side, where feces would leave my body in clear view. Releasing my bowels in this bag was difficult enough, for I remember waiting in lines for food or in check out lines at the grocery store, playing the fool when my body would make noises. The noise made when the stools released into my colostomy bag was a disgusting sound, one that most wished they had never heard. Of course, whenever that would happen, I would look around in a confused manner, sniffing in the air and looking at the person behind me with a disgusted expression. That seemed to work every time, and those who first looked at me understood that, of course, it was the person behind me who passed the gas. In time, I began to have a little fun with this, but sometimes, when my self-esteem was down, it would humble me, beckoning me to ask the question of whether or not surgery was really worth it. *Was it?*

One of the toughest things I had to deal with early in that surgical process was what happened frequently at night. Each shower I took was difficult, for I had to bandage and clean the open wound on my belly that was not allowed to heal for eight weeks. The reason it was not allowed to heal was because my body was healing from the other surgery, the one that removed the intestine. The reattachment of my small intestine to my rectum took place at the same time the removal happened, but it needed to heal before stools were able to pass through, which is why I had the bag. If I wasn't given that eight-week healing process, I would have become infected and an entire new set of trials would have been in my wake.

The showers themselves were not that painful, and the dressing of the wound was not the cause of my grief. What ailed me so was the trauma I experienced when I closed my eyes to sleep. When I was down, lying on my side for need of sleep, I was penetrated with nightmares and terrors of being in the hospital bed. When I would awake in the middle of the night, I would find, all too regularly, the sheets filled with loose stools that were supposed to be in my bag. My excrement would be all over, my colostomy bag ripped off of my wound, and the acidic stools covering parts of my pajama-clothed body.

Discouragement, humility, and confusion—these were the emotions that plagued me and found a home in my mind. Discouragement was the curtain that blocked the sun, humility was the refrigerator that fed my soul but dampened my spirit, and confusion was the wood and materials that formed the roof of my psyche.

The sheets would be covered in filth, and I would have to change them in the middle of the night, with sleep still on me. It happened so often during that eight-week period that I became numb to it. The stools would be so full of acid, because I now had no large intestine to process my food properly, that I would wake up with sores on my exposed skin. Eventually, I would be so tired at night, trying to recover from the hellacious surgery, that I wouldn't change the sheets anymore, but would sleep in my own feces. I was my own enemy, but I was so tired of it. I was scared, too, for fear had gripped me with the possibility that all of this pain giving me no better of an outcome than what I had previously experienced. I was down, I was exhausted, and I didn't care anymore. Passion for things filled me with dread, for there was such an absence there for any feelings whatsoever. Apathy was what consumed me and a sort of jaded disposition towards those who were positive in any way. Through the words and influence of various individuals, my naïve mind believed that everything was going to be okay, but I let the trials become my sugar that gave me energy in a bad way. I couldn't listen to anyone, though everyone around me was giving me their personal advice.

This advice is what harmed me the most, for I was told that I shouldn't have these feelings of anger and frustration towards God. If my faith was real, I would trust God in His plan, the perfect one, and that all of this was for my own good. *All of this was for my own good? So what part about the feces all over my bed, including on my face and in my hair, was supposed to be for my own good?* Those questions frightened me, for no one could give me a satisfying answer. It came to the point that people would give me their advice, however pathetically wrong it was, and I would tune them out. Ignoring them, letting my mind drift off to something else, I would smile and nod, knowing full well the extent of the hardness of my own heart. I had to come up with a philosophy in my mind that screamed over the loud and destructive words my "friends" would convey. I felt akin to Job once more; as he had to listen to the idiocies of his friends portraying their lopsided truth, so I had to do the same.

The Fourth of July was hailed as a celebration as I found myself up in Mammoth Lakes, residing in a home not my own. With the bag still attached to my side and feeling like a pig amidst sheep, I had my fill of elk burgers and beans galore. A set of fireworks and hours later, I retired to my bed that was sorely missed for want of sleep. Then it hit me; the most pain I have ever experienced, and the most pain I will ever feel sought me out that night. I had my own fireworks display going off in the midst of my stomach and intestinal lining. I was passing a stone; I was giving birth; I was having a heart attack; I was dying of cancer; I was all of these, for the pain consumed me. I experienced pain, like no other, at its very core. Little by little, as the beans made their way through the lining of what was left of my digestive track, my small intestine began to twist and turn, blocking any flow of movement. When this happened, I would have buildup within the confines of my less-than-normal intestine, and pain would jolt. As this continued, and as the small intestine would stubbornly refuse any leeway of movement, I would be engulfed with terrible discomfort.

Two hours after the beginning of my torment, my small intestine stopped digestion and began to develop gangrene. Inside my body, there began a war that I was losing terribly; circulation was getting cut off from what would keep me alive. Like a boa constrictor, my small intestine found its prey in me and beckoned me to die. The pain continued so intensely for thirty-six hours that, by the end of it, I was completely wiped-out and exhausted.

So those hours were a baptism in pain for me, flinging me through mud and fire, piercing my heart, but not necessarily breaking me. I was alone, as hopefully most twenty-year-olds are at night, and can remember the blankets that covered me. Like a quilt, they were my walls of defense against the shards of ice and missiles that were thrown at me. I tried protecting myself with a heating pad, for in the past, whenever I became ill with pain in my abdomen, I could always resort to that for some relief. Not so that night, for nothing brought any comfort.

Running to the bathroom every five to ten minutes to try and pass something through, knowing that I didn't even need the toilet because of the bag but doing so out of hope and more hope, I resolved to deal with the pain. After all, look what I had been through; I didn't need anybody else's help, did I?

Of course I did, but in my stubbornness and pride, I delved into my mind for strength.

Early the next morning, I was at my wits' end, for I was exhausted and beat and tired of everything. The culmination of my grandfather's death, my colon disease, my liver transplant, my parents' divorce, countless trials concerning my intestine, and now this left me jaded beyond belief. I had come to a place in my mind that left me no assurance or any feelings of emotional comfort. I wanted death to come upon me, hoping for that sweet sleep of cloudless nothing. I concluded that this new process—the process of having my large intestine removed, what I thought to be my victory—was indeed a failure. I felt I played right into the enemy's hands, and I

daydreams // an end to my nightmares

was dumbfounded. More than that, my spirit was crushed, crushed beyond any possibility of restoration.

The sun, the most beautiful sun, the strengthening sun, had finally set in my life. *Lord, take me now.* I got down on my knees, throwing off the walls of comfort that were my sheets, and prayed a very simple prayer. *"Lord, I earnestly pray, take away this pain, and bring me home. Let me die tonight, for I can't go on like this."*

Some people ask me whenever I speak, "Why didn't you go to the hospital to alleviate the pain?"

You must understand, the hospital, to me, was a symbol of the immense pain already in my life, and I had serious faith issues when it came to that place. That structure that hails a good and reputable name, the place that proclaims wellness and relief, was to me a shark in murky water. I felt like it always made me worse in order to make me more complete, better in some way. I felt as if it always took chunks of my life away, taunting me and promising relief when, in fact, I never became better. In short, the hospital scared me, for it always gave me bad news. It told me that I was dying, that I would never be the same again, that I would have to take medication for the rest of my life, that I wouldn't have to deal with other things if some measures were taken. The hospital was not a place of healing for me, but a reason for dying, a reason for death, an excuse for it. It represented death to me, and succumbing to it would be giving up. Interesting, but I gave up anyway that night, or I came the closest I have ever come.

More hours passed into the night, and then four o'clock in the morning came, slowly, like a walker in a marathon. Somewhere in the past, I had heard a lie that you could alleviate pressure in your abdomen if you vomited. My one-track mind, focused on the pain alone, took up this psychotic mission.

After walking to the bathroom, I shoved my index finger down my throat and heaved with a determined passion to see the contents of my stomach swimming in a toilet bowl. Trying this five more times, I gave up on that folly and started bawling. I was crying, crying because I didn't have the answers, crying because of everything I had been told, crying because vomiting gave me no comfort or release. I literally crawled back to bed, and as I lay there, slumped over, I wanted to rip the bag off of my stomach. I became violent, hitting the bed as if it had wronged me grievously, but I found that it only expended the energy I needed to survive.

I looked around my room then, trying to survey my life. The DVDs on the T.V., my bookcase, the slanting ceiling of a somewhat A-frame house, my computer cabinet, and the letters my girlfriend had given me were all trophies of another life. I couldn't remember what it was like, why I was smiling in the pictures I had, for I had only known pain. So tired, so confused, I searched for meaning behind what I was going through. Finding nothing, straining my ear to hear the God of creation speak to me as He did Moses through the burning bush, nothing came still. God was silent, God was still.

I threw off my covers, yelling at God; I walked through the hallway to the other room upstairs. Why was this happening, why wasn't the pain going away? Was it really necessary? Was it really for my own good? I looked to the glass door that was my last bastion of strength before the outside world, unlocked it, and stepped out into the cold biting air. The balcony, that sweet balcony that could collapse and send me home. *Okay, Lord, I am going to make this easy on You, when I step out on this balcony, cause it to collapse, sending me to my death.*

Seeing my breath, was it all for naught? After all that we had been through, God, am I going to die here? Yet I can't handle it anymore, take me home, now!

Impatience overran me as I began jumping up and down, hoping for the impossible—that the strong balcony would fall. No longer hoping for good—for the pain to go away—I hoped for death, or for the pain that would lead to death. When you reach that point, nothing else matters, for the pain consumes you, and nothing else can consume your mind. I loved life, but my life did not love me, so I felt that it was time for me to go home.

Can you imagine? I was actually jumping up and down, praying for death, trying to "help" God to take my life away. What kind of thinking is that? What kind of twisted theology would allow for that kind of logic? Yet there I was, at four o'clock in the morning, jumping up and down on an old balcony that would never falter under my heavy weight of a buck fifty. Each jump created more pain in my abdomen, so I soon stopped and collapsed on the splintered wood. Crying more tears, I was determined to "help" God, and I went inside. Another thought came to me, and that was to walk up and down the stairs with my eyes closed, praying for God to trip up my feet that I may fall and break my neck. Instead of alleviating the pain, it came upon me even more through my circus act of death, and my calves slowly began to cramp from the hundred or so flights I ascended and descended. What a sad, sad state I was in, trying to "help" God—the one who sent His Son to die for me that I might live—kill me. Yet there I was, a theology student, a philosophy major, a studied child of God, broken and destroyed. My belief remained, yet my faith in a sovereign Lord crumbled with each wince of pain, with each portion of torment I was asked to bear.

DAYDREAM

The roar of the crowd consumed my ears as my familiar tune began to play. Surveying what was before me, I entered the chasm of electricity and eager expectation and felt the soft glow of satin against my skin. The gloves on my hands were a bright red, weapons of destruction and chaos. I was wearing a belt around my waist, though for the life of me couldn't figure out why I was blessed to be able to wear it.

A champion's belt. Feeling the jolt of adrenaline surge through my veins, I took my first step into the crowded coliseum and began the long march down to the ring, the place where I was hailed for victory.

The odds were in my favor, twenty to one, but as I reached the ring, I saw the announcer shadowed by my opponent, and a twinge of nervousness hit me. Reeling, I almost threw up, but held down the liquids for fear of upsetting the mob. My trainer, though unknown to me now, stood on the bottom two ropes and held the last two high, making an easy entrance into the ring. Bouncing up and down with my gloves close to my side, I stared my opponent right in the eye, knowing victory was in my grasp.

My record was shady, but I always seemed to come out on top with a knockout or a favorable decision. This time, however, since the odds were so greatly in my favor, I was expecting more of a landslide victory. The announcer made his comments as we squared eye-to-eye, taunting each other with our menacing glares.

"In this corner, weighing in at one hundred and fifty pounds is Daniel 'Liver Boy' Parkins!!" *The crowd went wild, with the police and security barely able to suppress the roar of energy.*

"And in this corner, weighing in at two hundred and forty-five pounds, Joe 'Promises of no pain in Dan's life' McNutt!!" With confidence, I raised my fists and pounded his, oblivious to the overwhelming fact that he was a hundred pounds more than my body weight and six times my body strength. But I didn't have to worry about it; everybody couldn't be wrong. All I had to do was hang in there for the first couple of rounds and I would be okay, winning with a split decision, victory secured. So my trainer put the mouthpiece where it belonged, and the bell that signaled the beginning exploded with a loud clang, and the crowd at hand erupted in a piercing roar.

I stepped closer, counting in my head the seconds that marked the end of the first round. We danced in the ring for a while as I threw petty shots at his right eye. Recklessly, I threw the first punch, landing a damaging blow; wait, no . . . I only hit his glove, as he blocked my mosquito punch to the side like a paper doll. No, it was more like a leaf falling from a tree as my feeble attempts for penetration failed time and again. Was he toying with me? We heard a pounding on the mat that signaled the near end of the first round, and we both eased off a bit, clearly intimidated by each other. Right.

While my trainer proclaimed his plan for victory—yelling at me to dance around my opponent with no fear—I spit into the bucket. I had swallowed some water to clear my mouth, and now I saw that I had spit almost pure blood into the white bucket. Horror filled me as I looked at my opponent, my boxing nemesis, and I filled my body with as much

water as I could hold. Ringing, the bell taunted me, laughing at me as
it continued to pound in my ears. Just a few more rounds, and victory
was mine. After all, everybody had said that I was going to win, surely
not everyone would be wrong.

Toe-to-toe, we squared off one more time; but this time, he swung
away, making my face and stomach, scars and all, a sock torn apart by
a strong yellow lab, leaves burned in a fire, flesh pounded and destroyed
by a skilled warrior.

Who was I kidding? The first punch landed square on my left eye,
rendering me half blind and in pain. The second punch spewed out my
insides as it first hit my stomach and penetrated the back of my spine.
Powerful was my enemy, powerful enough to destroy me. Silence filled
the entire building as this boxer, this seasoned soldier, ripped apart
every fiber of my being, destroying everything I held dear. It was so sad
and pathetic, people began to cry. Why wasn't my trainer throwing in
the towel?

I ran around the ring, trying to avoid the now seven-hundred-
pound gargantuan giant hell-bent on destroying me. Was I just blind to
his size, or did he grow? Was I deceived from the very beginning? Why
didn't I see those claws of pain before, why didn't I see his armored skin
that was impossible to penetrate, even with bullets fired from a gun?
In seconds, he had me on the ground, pounding me left and right with
those weapon-like hands, pulverizing my every move and every sinew
of muscle and strength. I was shattered, and at that moment, all hope
was lost. I closed my eyes and accepted the fate which I was expected
to go through, the pain that was my lot. I despaired, and with that, I
passed away, losing all of my title, that belt I was wearing, and all that
represented me. I was famished and decimated, completely dissolved
and ruined.

CONTINUED SLEEP

Hours passed, and the pain grew more intense. Like birth pains
coming and going, so were these excruciating pains. "Excruciating"

only began to describe the feeling as my intestines twisted more and more, and, as I could only guess, became blacker by the minute. My stepsister was next door during all of this time, for she resided comfortably with us in that love-filled house; she woke up during one of my howling fits. I was screaming now, or more like a low howl, trying to get over this pain. It wasn't going away, and my attempts to "help" God proved to no avail.

My sister, Kirsty, ran downstairs after surveying my situation and woke up my mother. She did so despite my protests, and my poor mother once again came to my side. What could she do?

Though the feeling of pain did not subside with the aid of my mother, her presence encouraged me. I was able to express my utter torment at the situation, how I hated God and couldn't understand why He was letting all of this happen. With tears in her eyes, she couldn't answer my questions, and we both wept. A few more hours passed, and we were into the morning, and yet, to my horror, the pain had not passed. Sleep was not an option, so my body was without a single shred of energy. The hurt was so intense that I couldn't lay down. But, and this is a big but, I did not have the energy to stay erect in bed. So my mother came to my side and held me up, supporting the body weight that I could not. Can you picture that? My mother held my destroyed body up, amidst my drool and shouts of pain. More than that, it was as if she held up my faith for me, holding fast to the truth of God and what He was doing through me. I didn't see it then, for there was no way that I could. But I see it now, and I praise God for the gift of my mother, and what she did for me and with me.

At the end of it all, after my mother pleaded and after my skin turned a disgusting pale white, they carted me off to the hospital in town. I was completely distraught as they shoved a tube down my nose to relieve the pressure that had built up from the lack of bowel movements and such coupled with the fact that they gave me enough drugs to put an elephant to sleep. They themselves had no idea what to do with me, for I was like a treasure find to the doctors in Mammoth. They looked in their medical books voraciously, seeking out clues as to how to treat me. At the end of it, they threw up their hands without hesitation and called the hospital where I had had all of the surgeries. Within one hour, I was emergency-evacuated to UCLA hospital via jet airplane, with my mother faithfully riding in the cockpit. The drive alone on a day without traffic took over six hours, so needless to say, it was a rush. I remember none of the airplane ride, for the drugs did their dutiful effect, yet, I have glimpses and memories that are, to me, like photographs, still pictures of scenes of despair.

I praise God for that emergency evacuation, for the moment I woke up and became coherent, they told me that my liver was failing, and that if they hadn't caught it in time, I would have been much worse off. Try to imagine that for a second if you could. All the pain, all the hurt, all the immense frustration, only to find out that through it all, my liver was actually in major trouble as well.

I remember seeing Doctor Goldstein come into my room with a worried smile, admitting that he had made a mistake concerning my examination. It seems as though the levels of enzymes in my blood were elevated but never acted upon. For most of the summer, I believed I was fine, only to realize now that my liver was being attacked by my own body, destroying the very thing that could keep me alive.

The removal of my large intestine was the least of my worries; though if not for that night of torment, I would not have found out this even more terrible news, and I might have been thrown back into the mix of liver transplantation.

Was that what God was doing as He allowed me to go through that immense pain and suffering? That didn't make sense to me, but still, coincidence isn't to be found in the Good Book, though trust in sovereignty is. Another question that I felt would probably not be answered anytime soon.

My stay at the hospital was uneventful, and perhaps so monotonous as to be a bore. Still, a bore can be a good thing sometimes, for I was ready to leave by the fourth day. Each time the host of doctors gazed into my room to discuss the prognosis of my condition, I would act as cheerful and corny as possible, making jokes and having a good time. I didn't fool anyone, and by the fifth day, I was required to have a shunt—a tube that drained some of the bile out of my liver into another bag—put in my side. Another bag, another alien so attached as to make its nest on my pale and sickly skin, impregnating me with thoughts of disease and discomfort. I would now have two bags protruding from my insides, draining the little life I had left. At twenty years old, I was quickly becoming an old man, carrying around my "oxygen" from one place to another, diseased and decrepit.

My girlfriend was a dream to me, supporting me and loving me despite my inadequacies. She loved me all the more whenever I needed my dressings changed, whenever I needed a hug, whenever I needed her to hold my sick and disgusting laboratory of a body. I was losing weight fast, and my skin was as pale as a ghost in mid-morning's stride. I was weak and without esteem, yet she lifted me up higher than I was able to be before, loving me and making me feel more special than a favorite son. She was not only an angel, but a savior figure to me—if I can say that without being sacrilegious—for she brought me through a depressing time and gave me a gift that still lingers today. She gave me her heart, and in those precious few weeks that followed, we shared a hallowed love set apart from most. We shared the dreams of lovers unable to love, the essence of everything we were.

At the end of the eight-week period, and as I was getting used to the constant sheet changing in my bed, my colostomy bag was finally taken off, and I was able to go to the bathroom like everyone else again. Praise God in everything; praise Him in the highest, for I was able to feel the sweet cold of porcelain against my body once more as I released my bowels. Never again will I take that small gift for granted; never again will I succumb to the numbness of that tiny feat. It is the little things that count when you have nothing else, and it is those little things that make up what we like to call happiness. I knew, after the first night's rest without having to worry about losing my bowels in bed, that I had made it over a major hurdle in my life; a major victory had been won. I knew, and finally saw, a little glimpse of light in my life that had been enshrouded with darkness, surrounded in black, covered with filth. I knew that I was well on my way to recovery, for this was the last thing that I was going to have to deal with, right?

The reattachment of my small intestine to the beginnings of my rectum was difficult, in fact more difficult than I thought it was going to be, and left me squandering for energy and strength. I had to promise not to lift anything over five pounds for another eight weeks, and nothing over fifteen pounds for twice as long. It was indeed a difficult process, and truth be known, I was in the gym lifting weights way before the allowed period of time. I thought that I was a quick learner, and the battles that I had won in my mind proved to be a stepping-stone that encouraged my health and quickened my recovery.

A week out of the hospital, I slung my backpack on my shoulders and headed to college, only to learn that my feeble and weakened body wasn't ready to do so, dropping my hopes of a degree once again and leaving school to snowboard full-time in Mammoth. Well, at least, that is what I told my college buddies as I humbly dropped another semester of school. It was just too difficult to bear, and I decided early on that I had been through enough pain in my life, that it was stupid to needlessly go through more. I dropped out that year, my would-be junior year, hoping to recover physically, spiritually, and emotionally. Mammoth proved to be a salve for all three, a healer welcomed to my core, and a soothsayer of biblical proportions. Thank God for Mammoth Lakes and the mountain that takes its name.

change

She just came in, with her beautiful blue eyes that change color like the tide with each shifting blue she wears and hair just darkened closer to her natural color. A smile so deep and comforting, shining forth and beaming as to take my breath away, she looked at me, and I melted. On my lap, she wraps her loving arms around me, comforting me with those eyes and with that embrace, knowing full well what I have been through, for she herself has been through most of it with me, by my side. With tears in my eyes from just writing that last chapter, I realized what I had been through, and as I write these words, Kelly once again comforts me like no other.

The situation was traumatic, to say the least, for I have seen the depths of despair reach across and strive to drag me deeper still, beckoning me on as a lighthouse to a ship. Yet here I am, pouring out my life one detail at a time, picking apart the things that could bore and tickle the muscles to put this book down, and also wondering just how detailed I should make it. Should I let you in on how weak I really am? Should I tell you how pathetic my life has thus far been? Yet what do I have to hide, what do I have to say that could break me worse than the mere trials I have been plagued with?

So here I go again, another chapter of my life, one that still affects me today, one that still will affect me tomorrow. As each chapter in this book builds on the next, keep in mind the fact that this book only spans the past eight years of my life. Eight long years, eight terrible years, but eight years of the most daunting schooling I have ever seen or been a part of. My schooling goes on still, and the dreams are easily distinguishable from reality now, yet it wasn't always so. But in this chapter, the chapter of forgiveness, I found a grasp on my sanity, and everything began falling together. Granted, as time went on in my life, I was ripped apart some more, yet herein I found sanity in the emotional state. My physical body was destroyed countless times since, yet my spiritual and emotional person began a healing, leaving almost no scar or trace of what I had been through; only a memory of stories long ago.

T Boz was the name the restaurant where I found myself in the midst of a shouting match. Words, though having no physical form, injure and harm more than any other weapon when produced from the mouth of loved ones, when formed from the lips of a son to a father. There I was, eating a "chicken-fried-chicken" served with cucumbers and tomatoes in a balsamic dressing, searching for the door in hopes of a retreat. My father sat across from me with his beautiful and young girlfriend—the woman who would eventually take the place of my mother's position in my father's life—by his side. She became to me, later on in life, a blessing in her own right. But at that moment, she was a source of hurt, confusion, and betrayal. In my black and white mind, I knew one thing, and that was the crippling fact that my father divorced my mother, and now he was trying to convince me of the complete innocence of his actions that had left residual damage in my mind.

For so long I had had images and memories of hate and disgust towards the man who helped form my being, the man with whom I remember playing catch in the backyard, the man who used to hug me before I went to sleep, and the man who used to kiss my mother good night. These were memories that had now become dreams, and those dreams were overshadowed now by the nightmares of divorce thrust to the forefront of my thoughts. I think most of the reasons for my anger now stemmed from a feeling of betrayal at the very core, betrayal by the man I looked up to and admired more than any other. At my young age before the divorce, dare I say that my father held more of an importance than my heavenly Father? This was truth, and when I heard that he was having an extramarital affair with a woman over twenty years younger than him, younger than my oldest brother's own wife, red invaded my vision.

Each day I would retract from that relationship, little by little, as my mother, in her convinced mind, spoke doubt and anger into my own life, telling of his affair as if it was truth beyond doubt. As I have become closer now with my dad, I hold those statements with uncertainty and confusion, knowing now that they matter not, for have I not done much worse to my Father in heaven?

I think back on what I felt my dad did to me and my life, causing me to become a statistic relatively early because of the divorce; I can't help but look at my own life and my own actions towards the One who breathed life into my lungs. Have my actions not proved to be a catalyst for someone else's own statistic? Have I not myself wounded someone deeply, somehow possibly unknowingly? Have I not done this to God Himself? Pathetic humility rings in my ears as I am shoved to the ground, knowing that what I do *daily* to God puts chasms of air between us. Worse than that, I deny Him with my actions, yelling, "Crucify" louder than anyone and ripping His skin apart on the cross with each refusal to submit my own will.

Most people in this world are quick to point out the hardships that befall them or the torment they receive from others, yet are blinded by their particulars and ignorant of their own unworthiness. Yet that state of unforgiveness was my home for more than a few years after the divorce as I sat on my throne of self acknowledgment, comparing for the sake of judgment. I was my own worst enemy.

Worse still was my lack of forgiveness towards a fellow child of God, towards my own kin. That action alone showed my falsity in knowledge of the Holy One and what He gives me freely, for it was as if I held my father under my own thumb, beckoning him to prove his

daydreams // an end to my nightmares

worthiness to me. What right did I have in doing so, as if I had the power to forgive anyway, or rather, the power to withhold forgiveness? When I thought about it honestly in my heart of hearts, did I have any right to be unforgiving? I felt this pseudo-righteousness that gave me the authority of some pragmatic theology, yelling in the face of love as if a spirit controlled my actions, blinding me to the truth for which the gospel itself stands. And for so long, I spoke hate and anger to a man who only wanted my love, to a man who only loved me despite my incorrect assertions.

Stubborn, too, to the idea of loving my father again, I came to him only when I needed something from him. Wounding him deeply with each conversation, he would love me beyond understanding, as Hosea loved his prostituted wife. As I think back now, I see compassion exuding from my father, as if he held me in his arms of love as I ravaged his arms with my claws as a cat in frenzy. For the three years following the divorce, I grew to hate my father with an unholiness far beyond me, seeing in the midst of it a true love that gave me an example of Christ's own love for me. My dad was the example I needed in order to see what it was like to be loved unconditionally, despite my anger and protests and hurtful actions. No doubt I had done far worse to my heavenly Father, yet, to a degree, my dad showed me a love that never failed. Now one can argue that he did it out of guilt and shame, knowing that he was in the wrong and that he needed to love me, but is that true? I don't think so, because as time went on, he could have become jaded to my constant scarlet letter I threw upon his chest.

Divorce is a terrible act that throws everyone involved into a whirlwind of torment and leaves questions unasked and the answers encumbered in the web of lies. My friend Sai succinctly mentioned the relationship between the marriage act of humans and the marriage Christ has with His Church, but I feel I must elaborate on that truth. How many divorces happen in the United States alone? How many Christian families are ripped apart from the influences of our culture that sorely lacks integrity? How many bonds are broken as we usher in each season of hopeful renewal? How heartbroken and ashamed is our Christ who died for our sins, beckoning us to live not as the world? My one question to those who are going through a divorce is this: What if Christ treated the church, His bride, as you treat your spouse?

As the bride of Christ, does He have the will to divorce us if things are not going the way He originally intended? Does He sit back and weep as He hears of our sexual conquests in the world, our adulterous affairs with what we are enslaved to? Does Christ say in His heart, because of our infidelity, "I can't take it anymore, the betrayal goes too deep?" I have a close friend who is currently ambushed by the worst thing that could ever happen to a man. His wife of many years had an affair before his eyes. Undercover, my friend followed his unfaithful wife throughout an entire night, watching her every move with a man outside the bonds of their marriage pushing the start button on a blender that housed his heart. Such turmoil, such utter anguish as he watched her exit the demon's lair, walk to her car and drive home as if nothing ever happened. My own heart bleeds for him as I attempt to help alleviate the burden of sorrow now attached to his beating flesh. And as I draw away from the moment our conversation turns to tears, I see and hear in my mind the mirror played out before me that is my own life. *I am* that unfaithful wife to the Holy One to which I am betrothed.

I, in my own selfishness, play the role of the unfaithful wife every day, shadowed in my mind by the thought of an omnipresent God watching my every move, giving me opportunity upon opportunity to escape the temptations before me. I pull a lesson from the tragic story I listen to, guilty of the fact that therein I find my every move. How can I hold my father underneath my thumb and say "sinner!" when I myself have been living that life for far too long now? And as my father is part of that wonderfully tainted bride of Christ, is He saying to my dad, "No more, I can't take it, for the hurt is more than I can bear"? Is God saying in His perfect love, "Divorce is necessary, for I cannot forgive it anymore"? Now the question falls on my pathetic lap, encouraging me to love not as the world, but to forgive as I am forgiven. Forgiveness is the underlying trait that God

daydreams // an end to my nightmares

uses to pump the blood into our adulterous lives, and mercy is His eyes to turn away from the view He has of us as we walk out of the doorway of our infidelity. How could I not forgive my dad as he hurt my family and me? How can I not love him as a sinner like me? When Christ boldly claims in His loving voice to pull the plank, the gargantuan piece of wood, from our own sleep-swept eyes, to cast the first stone upon the sorry excuse of His creation, can I not look at my own life and see the tarnished finish before me?

As any sin is terrible to behold, and the sin of divorce is somewhat more extreme than others from our human vantage point, I can say with confidence that the sin of unforgiveness is far more destructive indeed. Though my father wounded me deeply by his actions, my stupidity in unforgiveness did far more damage. With the proper perspective, forgiveness not given is love not found. If I don't forgive him for what I feel he did to me, though in truth he only did it against God, then I know not love. The apostle John says in 1 John 4.7–8 to "*love one another, for love comes from God. Everyone who loves has been born of God and knows God. Whoever does not love,*" as John finishes, "*does not know God.*" Therefore, God is nowhere in him. What does society think, and what was I thinking when I was deceived into the mindset of unforgiveness? I did not and still cannot accept what he has done, nor will I ever agree with it, but I do know that I love him more now than I ever have, and the healing power of forgiveness and love has superseded a life that was filled with hate and confusion. My father now has come to be my best friend, outside of Kelly, and knows more about my life than any other person. He and I are so close, I even thought about asking him to be my best man in my wedding. I am blessed to be a part of my dad's life and blessed to have him in mine.

The summer after my junior year in college, the year which should have been the beginning of my major studies, my eyes turned yellow once again, and the flood of emotions almost overtook me. Yet again, the turmoil of change and uncertainty was the puppy nipping at my heels, the citrus as I bit into the orange of my life. The yellow in my eyes had plagued me as a virus contained in a microscope, barely visible to the naked eye, though blazing under the scrutiny of my own fears and perplexities. I could see the yellow come and go as I sought to hide my color of shame from those who knew me. Yellow was synonymous with disease, a road with which I was all too familiar, and every glare in the mirror each morning took me back to that hospital bed; it took me to the memories of weakness and hurt, confusion and pain, frustration and anger. Understanding my past, I tried finding strength in the peace of God that I had known briefly in my shadowed and murky past, the one ridden with its own torment of sickness.

But my past always found me again, as I would go to the grocery stores, hiding my eyes behind yellow lenses and never looking someone directly in the eye. Something different happened to me this time, however, for I ignored my problems and concentrated on living my life as joyously as possible, never giving full victory to the fears I held in my mind. I knew the road that was before me, if it truly meant that I was sick again, sick from the disease that almost killed me before. But this time, instead of fighting my condition, fighting the fact that I was different, and fighting the empty words of all who proclaimed the negative yellow in my eyes, I embraced it. Instead of getting angry at anyone who spoke of the jaundice in my eyes, I would admit and tell of the love of God and how He had given me a peace. That peace was in fact truth, for as I embraced my life and all of the confusion with it, as I did not fight the will that was acted out before me day to day, I released something.

Release is not easy, and I believe it can only happen after many duels of defeat, but therein I found some reality and some order to the life I called my own. In short, I released my will, my desires of a fruitful life, my strong hope of a life of normalcy, and finally embraced the trials. One could ask me, "Is that giving up?" Absolutely not, but it is giving in. I gave in to the fact that I was indeed sick, that I had indeed gone through terrible trials. I gave in to the truth that all was not okay with me, that the lies proclaiming health were somewhat absurd, and I found peace in God. I sought out His sovereignty, His control, and found faith in His perfect plan for me.

Releasing my will to His was huge in my life, though I believe it could not have happened had I not realized my unforgiveness for my father. For in that unforgiveness I found the first foundational truth that I was a hopeless, wretched person hell-bent on accomplishing my own will with my own agenda. Realizing my sin and need for a perfect Savior that died for me, I saw finally that my plan for my life was somehow misconstrued as well. How could I know what was best for me, though I fought it tooth and nail for so long thinking that I did, when I didn't even know how to love properly? Who was I in my own mind, with my pride seething and bubbling out the top of every action and reaction in which I found myself?

It really wasn't difficult to understand the trials that caused the pain in light of my own humanity. You see, I was trying to make logic out of God, holding to my own earthly presuppositions that said—along with the culture that so influenced me and the false theologies at specific churches along the way—that I deserved the MTV life that would be vivid in my vision daily.

The armor I held close to my heart, the protection the Holy Spirit gave me as I headed next into what seemed to be the inevitability of another liver transplant, was the open mind of allowing God to work in my life. It was the idea that I didn't have all of the answers, and that the speed bumps along the way may not make sense since my headlights had been out for so long. This was the truth that got me through each night. In fact, holding to the idea that it was not imperative to have all of the questions answered like ducks in a row, I was able to form some sort of hope that God, a personal entity far beyond my finite thinking, was indeed in control and I was not.

So with Christ truly as my cornerstone for the first time in my life, I went to the doctor with a resolve not my own. I had been living in Mammoth, realizing each day was another sick opportunity to live for myself, and doing so blindly and well, I found this new truth of God's sovereignty as the comfort and washing of my licentious life.

Sitting in the waiting office was something I remember as an unholy experience, with the enemy attempting to knock me off with the crushing blows of people repeatedly reminding me of the color of my eyes. "Oh, you look really sick," they would say curtly. In my reply, I would say, "Oh really? Gee, I didn't know that, for it is not like I see my ghostly reflection in the mirror every morning. Thanks for pointing that out." As my sarcasm would unavoidably seep out louder than the color of my disease, I would ignore the assailant and slip back into the magazine or book of theology that had previously caught my attention.

Tests beyond tests faced my diagnosis; afraid, yet securely awaiting the onslaught of news, I found out that fateful Friday morning that I did indeed need another transplant. I was dying again, and the telltale signs of elevated liver functions and yellow eyes were indications of such. Walking out of the doors of the UCLA hospital with the crusted gel from the ultrasounds still clinging to my skin, I made the lonely drive to Mammoth Lakes once more, lost in the music that helped me worship the God I sought for solace. *"Lord, my faith in You is all I have now, take me, drive me as I do this car, to the place I need to go."*

That next Sunday's worship service was one I will always remember, along with so many other events that have become deeply rooted in my memory, as my mother and I both stood up to tell the congregation about my need for a new life. Tears flooded Church on the Mountain as my mother first spoke of our undying faith in the God I now serve and her unshakable trust in His sovereign plan. Clinging to her beneath my arm and close to my heart, I began my speech with silence and resolve. "I *will* be okay, and I now know that though I may not understand what God is allowing, I do know that I am His child." My voice began to quiver then, as memories of the first transplant clouded my vision like a storm. All the pain, all of the uncertainties, became a deluge in my mind, attempting to wash away my hope in God. "I know that He is going to take care of me and see me through even this."

As tears trickled down my soft yet sunken cheeks, yellow eyes blazing like a sickened sun, I ended with this admonishment: "We must stand firm in our faith, whatever our circumstances may be. And it is time for me to practice what I preach, to put to the test the words I read in the Bible every day. Pray for my health, but pray for my strength." I felt like a warrior going to battle, prepared now more than ever, and confident in my promises of sonship. *What would you say? Can you imagine?*

The first few days of that week were spent in solitude in my room, unable to remove myself from the fact that I was going to either die or visit that home away from home once more. Another year, another set back, another time wasted when I would not be able to finish school. *Lord, not my will, but Yours.* This sucked, and I was truly scared to face what lay before me.

Wednesday, after hanging out with some of my friends, I had heard that there was a woman from Zambia, Africa coming to town who supposedly had a "healing ministry."

What? A "healing ministry" from where?

First of all, I had become so jaded to the amount of prayers and laying on of hands that I wanted nothing to do with her, and second, she was from where? But something was itching in my skin that night as friend after friend each proclaimed his or her willing excitement for such an opportunity to view someone with a healing ministry. In my false theology, I viewed this as close to heresy since I believed no person should be elevated beyond what God Himself gives them, but reluctantly and without support, I decided to go.

It was interesting that my mother, who was more excited than anyone about this woman, didn't urge me to go. I later asked her why, suspicious that there was some other motive causing her silence, but she knew my heart well and thought that I would definitely not go if she said so. Sad, but she may have been close to the truth. I had my relationship with God, a very private one that was still developing, and one that will develop till the day I die, but I felt the scratching of nails down a chalkboard whenever my mother tried to give me any "insight" into God or how He worked. This was stemmed from all of the innocent appeals she gave me, telling me that I wouldn't have to deal with each new trial and that each trial would be the last, and I would be wounded more than she could ever know when her idle words dug deep in my open sores.

So there I was, sitting in the back row of the congregation as we all worshiped together, giving voice to my reluctance when I would say boldly, "God doesn't need to use anyone to heal me, He can do it on His own. After all, He can use a donkey to talk to someone, He sure as heck doesn't need anyone from another country to heal me."

As she called up people from the audience, asking for those dealing with various disorders, ailments, and diseases, I waited patiently, secretly hoping that she would call a liver problem up. *"If she calls a liver problem up, then maybe I will consider." But, did someone tell her about me? Surely they did, but why wasn't she calling me forward? See, I told you, this whole thing was a hoax.* Satisfied, I lay back in my seat, slouched and ready for the end of the service.

As she ended her "healing" time, she went back to her guitar as she and two other women began to worship in their own language, which was truly beautiful. Before that happened, however, I saw a pillar in the front row in the form of my stepfather, Ed, jolt up from his seat. With a determined walk that only he could accomplish, looking as Moses no doubt did when God used him to part the Red Sea, he walked around the chairs heading straight for the back of the room. His gaze was determined and fixed on the floor, and as I lost him out of my peripheral, I dismissed him from my mind and concentrated on the songs before me. No more than a few seconds later, I felt his grip, strong like an ox, take a hold of my shoulder, yank me out of my chair, and begin dragging me forward. He was crying, loving me more in that action than I had ever felt before from anyone, giving me the strength I needed to accomplish what I had been contemplating in my heart. But what would people think? No matter now, I was halfway down the aisle when I felt everyone's gaze on the sick boy with a liver disease.

DAYDREAM

I can't say how old I am, for the hands directly connected to my body seem to be around thirty or so. Dirt and grime are underneath my fingernails, and I am digging. The dirt itself is fairly wet, and very compacted. Like digging in clay, it was a hard pan, offering me no benefit of softness. Each thrust I made gave very little progress, though ripped somehow some of my muscles as they worked hard to lift the shovel high and remove the dirt.

No matter how hard I worked to remove the dirt, I didn't seem to make any progress. For some reason, I have been doing this all of my life, and after thirty years or so, it seems to fit. This is my profession; this is what I was chosen to do. No water, no rest, just constant relentless digging with a shovel that is dull and bent. Is this fair? Well, I could be digging something else, something that smells which comes out of everything. So, I guess I can't complain . . . it could be worse.

Everywhere I look around me, I see other men and women taking rests in the shade, drinking lemonade or something of that sort, yet here I am, slaving away in the hot sun, getting baked like the cookies I so desired. How come I don't get a break? How come I work so hard and nothing seems to get any easier for me? Why do I have to constantly work in the sun all day—what is more, in the hard clay dirt—and everyone else gets to shovel in soft soil?

So many holes I have dug, and so many of those holes I have filled, and nothing to show for it. Only a few calloused hands and muscles stronger than most. Out of the corner of my eye, I see the Foreman. Should I ask him for a break? I see him giving others a chance to sit in the shade and have a wonderful rest with cool drinks to refresh their souls. He is smiling at me now, should I ask him for a break? Do I dare? I guess it can't hurt anybody. What is he going to say to me, "Get back to work"? I guess it is time to take my chances. After all, I have worked hard enough; he probably wants to bless me or ease this workload somehow.

For some reason, I am so afraid. I am so afraid that he is going to say no, and all of my expectations will come tumbling down. Those trees look so great to sit under, with the breeze slightly whisking away the sweat and the lemonade quenching the thirst that burns like a crackling fire. If I ask him for a break, what will he say? I am so afraid, I can't do it; I will just continue working and hope that he will take the initiative *to give me rest. Who am I kidding? It is time to take a chance, I don't care anymore. I need a break.*

CONTINUED DREAM

The woman, fittingly named Grace, had just asked if anyone would like prayer for anything. That had been the firecracker under Ed's seat that sent him flying for me. *What was I doing?* I had no idea, but what I did know was that, regardless of whether I wanted to or not, I was going forward to receive prayer. Silence filled the room as each person who had been there the previous Sunday and more, the people who had for so long fervently prayed for my healing, all fixed a rainbow of hope above my head. Ed could have brought me to one side of the small congregation of a hundred and fifty or so, but instead, he brought me smack dab in the frontal gaze of everyone, blocking Grace's view of her captivated congregation.

Without a word from anyone, Grace laid her right hand on my right shoulder, stating, "And Lord, in Your glory alone, I pray for this young man's healing."

The church, which had now become my family, hushed their agreements underneath their breath, with a couple of shouts giving me even more insecurity. *What was happening?* Then all of the sudden, I felt her right hand come to my head and her left hand on my shoulder, and she yelled, "In the name of Jesus Christ, the name with all power and authority, I pray a healing on this young man's liver! Heal it now, in Jesus name!" A boom louder than I have ever heard rang in my ears as the entire congregation in one accord yelled and praised God. Shouts above shouts, hope riding hope, I felt an incredible wave of emotion overtake me. I felt an immense surge of cold water or something, going from my toes out through my eyes as I wept like a little boy. No experience before or any since can compare to the feeling I received. The claps and the praises rang forth in the night as Grace called all of the young adults and kids to

daydreams // an end to my nightmares

the front. Hands were raised and the shouting consumed my ears as she continued to pray for our future ministries and the like.

Sneaking outside through the back door, praying that no one followed me but not looking back at the congregation for fear of seeing them actually on fire, I stepped out into the cold biting air. It was May then, and very cold, but I could see the Sierra Mountains before me and the starry sky above, beckoning me. Something happened to me then, for I could not stop laughing and crying. Laughing and crying, crying and laughing, praying with all of my strength from the bottom of me to the tip of my head, I hoped that it was true. *Was I healed? Was I healed?*

After the crying had stopped but the laughing had continued from the prospects of possibly being healed, I spent the next few days again not wanting to talk with anyone. I knew that I needed proof if anything had happened, and it just so happened that the hospital desired more testing to see how sick I really was. *Is it true, did it happen?*

That Friday I set out for UCLA Hospital again, this time with different expectations. How would you feel? What would you be thinking? All my life, all my seemingly long years of trials and pain, I had never received any hope, any gift that gave me encouragement in the form of health. *Could it be true? Don't question, Dan, just believe.* So I claimed healing in my mind, knowing and believing that God was fully capable to do so, yet never seeing it before.

The look on the doctor's face was priceless as he viewed that morning's blood results. What? How could it be?

"Mr. Parkins, we can find nothing wrong with your blood levels, but we think there may have been a problem with the results, so we need to take some more tests to confirm."

Could it be true?

One blood test, two ultrasounds, one CT scan and one very long MRI later, they told me that they couldn't find a trace of any scar tissue on my liver. They were so perplexed to see that I no longer needed a transplant; my liver was perfect. Perfect? It had never been perfect before, not even right after the first transplant. What do you mean perfect?

It was true, and despite the confusion on the faces of all the doctors and the commotion I raised, or rather, God raised, I had been healed. He had used a woman from Zambia, Africa named Grace Melinga to be His instrument of healing in a life that needed it so desperately. The news came as confirmation to what I had decided in my car on the ride down there—that I was indeed healed—and let flow the aqueducts of relief through every sense of my being. I wept until no tears would flow, and after I wept, I screamed for joy. After I had collected my feelings and prayed my prayers that this was no dream, one thought pervaded my mind. Finally, because of my earlier liver transplant and my somewhat lack of immune system due to my immuno-suppressive drugs, and after all this talk of never being able to leave the country, will I finally be able to fulfill my real dream of going on a mission trip to another country? This was what I so desired, this was something I was passionate about.

China beckoned me, and begrudgingly, the doctors consented, yet not before expressing their belief in my utter stupidity. What did they know, they were only doctors . . . right?

gifts

three weeks to go, and I had to come up with a sum of over four thousand dollars for my dream trip to China. Raising support for me was something I was not familiar with, though in truth I approached it with a naïveté that I think back upon with fondness. Never again have I ever had the overwhelming support of those friends of mine and the family members who all shared the trials in my life. In truth, God blessed me with over sixty-three hundred dollars in the matter of two weeks, which to this day I am still in awe over. Everyone told me that I would probably not be able to raise the support, but again, God proved them wrong. I saw myself as the miracle child now, one that avoided death with the mercy from the Creator, and felt more than ever like God's kid. Firmly set in His arms, I rejoiced in the newfound surge of faith. It was then that I truly felt like I could conquer the world for Christ, and I felt that China was the first place to do so.

The fear of death no longer had a hold on me, since I trusted that I was walking in God's perfect plan. God's sovereignty had new meaning to me as this seasoned soldier now set his scope on the most vastly populated culture ever—China, that body of land that held so many mysteries, the place with so much bondage to its religions which glorify earth and man. Was I really going to see the Great Wall that had plagued my dreams for so long, even more now than ever? For so long I wanted to travel to an Asian province, and for my entire life, I was denied this. This was due mostly to the mere fact that my immune system, ever since the liver transplant surgery, was a fourth of that of any "normal" person.

For the rest of my life, mind you, my body will always be attacking my liver as a foreign substance, and so the doctors never before gave me the clearance to travel across the seas. To this day, I am still forbidden to breathe the air south of our borders for fear of the dried human feces that ride on the invisible waves of air there. But now I was able to smell the freedom of travel, to make a claim, so to speak, for the God who healed me. But why did He do it now? Why did He heal me at this point in my life? It was not like I was complaining, but that question put me in distress as I took off from China Air or something similar to that.

Stopping in Vancouver with a small layover before we headed off to the great unknown, I felt like a little child again, back when I was six years old and only needing to worry about the time I came home from playing in the street in order to make dinnertime. After all, my Dad in heaven was taking care of me, and I was right where He wanted me. Did it matter that we could get into serious trouble for doing what we were doing? Heck no, for I heard it once and believe it now that the most dangerous place to be is outside of God's will . . . just ask Jonah. The safest place we could be in our lives might possibly be in the Sudan or in the towns of Afghanistan, as long as the most powerful God is on our side. I would rather be safe in my Father's arms doing what He wanted me to do, rather than taking the chance to be swallowed in the belly of a fish.

Stepping off of the plane with eager expectations, dripping with joy and uncertainty, we made our way to the check lines that were crowded with people from all different nations. Our first obstacle was getting our paraphernalia of smuggled Bibles and other Christian propaganda through the communist regime that faced us head on. The darkness we saw in the midst of those terminals did nothing to our hope as we saw men in uniform carrying what looked like fully automatic guns of destruction; they stared at me in particular because of my blond hair and extreme height compared to the average native of their land.

Making it through their lines of defense, our group, the hearty warriors sent from the United States as ambassadors of Christ, met our interpreters that had long been in relationships with our guide, a man full of integrity and wit. Gwynn was the name of our pastor and leader who took us fearlessly into a foreign land; he was a man who had been through more trials than most, and a man I respect more than most. Gwynn himself holds a special place in my heart as the quintessential missionary who travels to the unknown of different countries more times than he can probably count, trusting in God completely and fully. He is to me my ideal of Paul, though in truth, I wished I could be his Timothy or Titus, knowing that that possibility would be futile to wish for because of my condition. He took a huge step of faith bringing me along on his journey to penetrate a small province in China, if any province in China can be considered small, for my history of health had to be daunting. Nonetheless, he trusted in God that I was called to be a part of his team, and so he brought me along without any hesitation. He was excited for me to be there and to have his own daughter along for the first time, maybe not in that order. He kept me close by his side wherever we went, for he was like a shepherd to me. I was blessed with Gwynn on that trip, as anyone anywhere would be blessed to have him in their presence, and Sower's International, the missionary project he heads up, is the better because of him.

Our interpreters need to be mentioned as well, for what they do day in and day out in China, furthering the Kingdom of God, struck me boldly in the face early the first morning we arrived. Though we were strangers in their country, they welcomed us with a holy excitement explained only in that way, for they became to us a family while we were away from home. My roommate was one of the interpreters, and though he snored as the loudest saw cutting down the tallest redwood, he served God with incredible zeal. At that time, he had been previously in prison for his faith more than three times and since that time probably countless times. Here, I was so comfortable with my faith compared to the hardships he faced daily, and I realized that my pathetic testimony was one dealing with myself, not because of my stand for Christ. He has treasures in heaven far beyond imagination, and I look forward to seeing him, if that will be a possibility, in our future eternal state.

He was a short man, with scraggly hair and a jumbled mouthful of teeth, showing a smile as warm as my girlfriend's did at the time. He was wearing stereotypical glasses an inch thick, framing his round face and small eyelids. He was beautiful to me, possessing a face I will keep with me forever, a man I can only respect and pray for, and a soldier on the front lines proclaiming the same God I serve comfortably.

The trip was incredible, but there are more details than I could possibly describe in this book. However, there were three instances that changed my life forever, and I ask for patience as I attempt to describe them. They are in my heart forever, etched in the reserves of my mind on which I reflect quite often, pulling them out of the filing cabinets in my soul as a special picture in a frame. Without them, I would be a different person, and with them, my theology is that much more complete.

The first one took place when we were in the middle of the trip, after visiting the "sights" of China, such as the Great Wall and the Forbidden City. We had just started in on our missionary activity, attempting to visit the orphanages to just love on the little children who had homes of concrete and beds made out of the same material. We didn't get the okay to visit the orphans because of the date when we visited. It was June, if I remember correctly, and the date corresponded with the "anniversary," if it can be called that, of the massacre at Tiananmen Square. Security all around the provinces is always tighter around that time, and having a tall Caucasian enter their abode on such a date was seen as a possible starting of another revolt. Regardless of the fact that we wanted only to "love on" the orphans, we were greatly restricted, and our hope to be a part of their lives, even for such a brief time, was put on hiatus until we got clearance.

So, the first night in one of the smaller provinces was a chance to get outside on my own, living a fantasy I had planned from the beginning. I felt like Leonardo DiCaprio in his movie, *The Beach*. Though it wasn't Thailand, I set out at night, not knowing a thing about where I was or where I was going. Never before have I felt such freedom, such a lack of attachment to the life I lived back home, to the heartache I had experienced. My only companion that night was my God I was serving, and I was completely confident of my safety. Saying the only word I had learned in Chinese, "Hello," I smiled my cocky smile as I walked by the venders on the street selling an array of exotic food I could only gaze at. They weren't exactly my idea of clean, and so I walked by holding my breath from a fear I heard in the back of my mind. That fear was all too real as I could only imagine the doctors speaking their discontent with me even being there. But the smells were incredible; boy, were they something else. With each new sight, I drank in everything, taking mental pictures that I still have with me, quickening my pace away from the comfort of the hotel room. I wanted to see more; I wanted to feel more.

I experienced something that night as the strong glares and uncertain smiles reached my mind. Most of these people did not know the peace I had, the understanding that there was a God who loved me and loved them just the same. Something was crying out in my spirit, a feeling of sorrow coupled with my inexpressible joy of just being there. I saw mothers carrying their children or walking them by the hand, going about their business of survival. I saw teenagers playing games or smoking their lungs out on the street corners. I saw old men playing tile games and young men looking out for a woman to catch their eyes. I saw what I thought I would, for I saw my home there amidst the differing language and culture. I saw that I was in no way different than most of these people, for I saw beneath their eyes a need for something more. I saw a longing for meaning itself, and I felt as though I had the answer. But staying in my comfort zone and with the excuses of the language barrier, I maintained my silence as I walked by.

Something was born in me at that time that changed me, and that was my strong desire to do something with my faith, to share unashamedly the truth and the peace that I held in the confines of my mind. Part shame and part uncertainty, I made a vow to make a difference in the circles to which I would return. If I had this truth, the truth that made an immense difference in my life, the truth of the gift that I did not deserve, then why did I not share it?

In my selfishness, I made my way back to my room, enjoying little by little the new sights and sounds of China, with a trail of kids and teenagers trailing me for want of seeing something they had never seen before . . . a tall, white, blonde American male.

Because of that night, I went on to share my testimony through interpreters during that trip, seeing the fruit of the truth I proclaimed in the decisions of the Chinese who wanted to live for Christ. It was the first real time—and when I say "real," I mean actual commitments for Christ that went beyond a "feeling"—a true experience where I conveyed the gospel and hope of Christ to people who overwhelmingly accepted. Watching people come into my family from way across the globe produced in me a certain body dynamic I can't shake nor ever hope to. No matter what, those now dear brothers and sisters have been redeemed because of their faith alone in Christ Jesus and so have been set apart. Praise God, they are a part of His Kingdom, the one I am serving to further as I reside continents away. Sad, in a way, that over fifteen hundred denominations can't seem to buy a clue in this regard, always so "competent" in their specific, different theologies. Those theologies, by the way, I am assuming, are based on the very Word of God rooted from the original Greek, right? Can you catch my sarcasm? I don't want to get on my soapbox here, for that is an entirely different matter, something I will devote much of my life to, but there is a stark need for the body of Christ to come together. For as it is, the church doesn't even have legs to run the race we are called to run, and the distant memory of the oil in the lamps that should be shining is a vague hope of something that once was.

The second life-changing experience still makes me sad to think about, for it was at the most exciting part of my life, up to that point, when I saw the most horrendous crimes. Cement castles, much like the architecture of a person who had never been outside and knew only absolute boredom and non-comfort, were made entirely of walls of sadness. The steps we walked to the orphanage were light and free, having images of smiling children with certain expected naiveties happy to see us. But when we saw what human hands had built for defenseless children who had been orphaned from parents murdering parents and the like, we quickly became somber. Desperate to offer a glimpse of our heavenly Father above, we put on our pseudo smiles of happiness and walked with an air of hope and confidence.

Who were we kidding? Ourselves? The only English words these wonderful children knew were "Hello," and "I love you," and they spoke them more eloquently than anyone I had ever heard before. There was one girl there who went by the name of Wang Shin, and she stole my heart. In my journal, I spoke of her beauty and the fact that her little body of eight years old completely destroyed any rationale towards what I had known before:

Wang Shin. That was her name. Probably the most beautiful little girl I have ever laid eyes on. I was seriously debating on how I could support her if I adopted her, but I know that that isn't why God brought me to China. Wang Shin was a girl from the orphanage that I will always remember in my prayers, and someone who will always have a little piece of my heart. When I first arrived at the orphanage, we were greeted by a wonderful performance from the kids. They were so cute and I wanted to run up and hug them all. Soon after, we were able to play with them, Ring Around the Rosie, Duck Duck Goose and the like. The children didn't care, for they just wanted to be loved more than anything. One thing I will remember was their fascination with how tall I was and how hairy my arms were (which is nothing compared to most westerners, mind you). I felt bad because most of them were clinging on to me and fighting to hold my hand, hitting each other and such. Most of the kids were very violent with one another as well, except this one little angel. She took a hold of my two fingers and wouldn't let go . . . and I didn't either. Her features were so tiny and beautiful, and when she looked up at me with those eyes, I melted. She first took me around the play area made of cement, trying to communicate with me. I wanted everyone else to go away so I could spend time and hold this wonderful girl . . . she kept asking when I was coming back and if I could see her next time. Then, near the end of our two hour visit, she told me she loved me in English . . . I cried the entire way to the hotel, angry that I couldn't do anything about her situation.

Here in the comfort of my home, sitting on a chair that is worth more money than those kids will ever see in clothes or food, typing on a computer with a technology that would leave them breathless, I ask myself, "What am I complaining about?" Even in the hospital beds that became my home away from home, I had it better than those poor little children with dust and dirt-crusted cheeks. Is my thinking that selfish, that self-centered as to think I deserve any of it?

In light of the 9/11 attack on the Twin Towers, I look at all of the stickers of the American Flag on the backs of car windows and bumpers. A friend of mine succinctly noted one sticker in particular that said, "Proud to be an American." Excuse me, but we are so lucky and blessed to be born into this country. Do we not even take that for granted, also? Many people will read this entire story of mine and think it too radical, that the questions I raise do not apply. But is that so? Could it be that our hearts are so hardened at our present situations as to become numb to it all? How lucky are we? How lucky am I to receive liver transplants and other surgeries to correct diseases, yet I complain at those diseases like anyone else? What am I complaining about for crying out loud (I am standing on my soapbox again)? I am so blessed to live in a country that has the kind of medical capabilities that afford me a life I should have lost long ago. Do we ever stop to think about those things? We think that we deserve so much because we have had it for so long.

But I guess my main question, from a pastor's perspective that I am quickly forming, is, "Do we not treat Jesus and what He has done for us in the same light—like we deserve His grace?" In our American culture that I have been raised in and that I have been so incredibly blessed to be a part of, don't I myself view Christ in this same context, that I deserve His forgiveness? Give ear to me, for I will not be so bold as to actually claim that—nor would anyone else in their right minds—but those little children, in some way or another, showed me that I *live* like I believe it, even if I don't give words to that view. God, in some form or another, touched me miraculously through them, more than I could ever bless them by dunking on their basketball rims or how fast I could run in Duck Duck Goose. He revealed a little of my heart that day and broke it in a million pieces to be put back together by the love and blessings He showers me with on a daily basis.

Lastly, the third thing that hit me hard, only reinforcing this foundation-shattering theology, was when I visited a small village four hours from the nearest established community. The countryside was beautiful, with mountain tops flat as could be and hills that looked as though God was in a hurry to put them down because of their simple design. They looked to be perfect triangles with green hair at the bases and brown skin spotted with specks of rock all the way to the short top. We passed men and women toiling in the grueling sun with their water buffaloes and ancient farming tools, using what seemed to be every bit of that huge continent for rice and pastures. Two stops at local stores asking for directions took us to the place we needed to go; another excellent journey marked with incredible excitement and wonder. When our van stopped, silence consumed the car before the door opened to the fresh air, unspoiled by any hint of corruption, and our uncertain fears melted with the heartwarming smiles that greeted us.

The people of the village were decked in their traditional garb of bright colors and patterns which I could never do justice to while describing on paper. We met the "chief" of the village, who wanted to show us their ancient customs. Just as the customs were no doubt ancient, poverty itself was in rich supply. One shabby wire produced only the amount of electricity to light a bulb, which could barely warm the family of cockroaches that took up residence on the floor, and that wire stretched for miles and miles in the northern direction. The village was beautifully simple, and our group stopped to take a picture.

The event that hit me and changed me forever was when we went to the village's festival "square" up in the trees above and partook in ancient marriage ceremonies and the like. It was overwhelming as the village sang to us and loved us unconditionally, having a roaring good time and stepping over branches that moved with the beat of a drum, covenantly finishing off the deed of marriage. I don't think that it was sanctioned by God, for even the girls in our group were getting "married" to other girls from the village. But it showed me the simplistic way in which that "family" in a village deep within the Chinese borders was able to laugh and enjoy themselves, despite the obvious lack of modern conveniences. When Christ bids me to take up my cross daily, my own instrument of death, to deny my own desires of the stupid material things that so consume my thinking, can I not do it? Did I not have the perfect example of a people so enthralled with each other, so loving and unselfish towards one another's hopes, that I myself can still desire things so selfishly? Be that as it may, even after I write this sentence, I know that I will fall right back into the very things I learned in China to suppress. *Dear God, I need you every day. Show me how to live like I really believe that.*

DAYDREAM

It was an old house, but for some reason it didn't creak and crack under the pressure of my five-year-old weight. Sweat was glistening off of my forehead from playing baseball with my Dad outside. Looking down at my shoes, I saw the freshly cut pieces of grass attached to my white shoelaces from all the running from one place to another on the lawn. It was wonderful. I was having the time of my life.

Reaching into the refrigerator, I pull out a Coke that quenches my thirst like no other before. The suds tickle the back of my throat, so I put it down on the counter. Sun is penetrating the kitchen window and shining onto the counter and floor, washing it anew. I can smell something so wonderful and tasty cooking in the oven close by, only dreaming of what it could be. This is nice; this is perfect. I have no worries, no concerns, only the need to fill my stomach with the source of that wonderful smell and to satisfy the healthy thirst I had worked up from playing outside with Daddy.

The screen door opens, and I hear bold footsteps enter from outside. "Daddy, what are You cooking?"

"Cookies, son, cookies to renew your energy."

"Can I have some soon?"

"In time, son; they are almost ready."

My mouth began to salivate in eager anticipation as He said those words. Dad was a giant of a man with huge hands and strong shoulders that showed His hobby of building things. Actually, He built everything as far as I can remember, sometimes getting His hands bloody from the effort. But somehow, I knew that that wasn't His profession, but I knew that He was the best at it. In fact, no one could build like Dad, no one.

As He reached the doorway to the kitchen, I first noticed His huge shadow cast on the floor of the room, almost enhancing the light shining through the windowsill. Dark thick hair speckled with shafts of gray danced about His head, with a crusted and weathered smile perfecting His glorious face. Looking down on me, He winked, and I ran to hug Him.

"You sure wore me out playing outside, Danny; what say you and I take a break and enjoy a couple of those cookies when they come out of the oven?"

"You bet!"

Grabbing the handle of the oven, I began to hastily pull the door down. "Wait Danny, let Me, you might hurt yourself."

"Okay, Daddy, but can you hurry? My stomach is making noises."

With a chuckle, He lowered the oven door and pulled the cookie sheet out, placing four cookies for each of us on paper towels. Then He grabbed the carton of cool milk from the refrigerator, poured both of us tall glasse, and sat down on the table. As He crossed His legs in relief, I jumped up on His massive thigh and ate to my heart's content.

"That is just what I needed, Daddy . . . let's go play some more."

"There are always cookies in the cookie jar, Danny, help yourself to as many as you want. And when we run out, I can always make you more. I can always make you more."

CONTINUED DREAM

After times of almost getting our passports taken away and being chased out of universities by the Secret Police, we reached home and vowed never again to take for granted the freedom we have at "Home." But China will always be in my heart, beckoning me to challenge the beliefs that are so evident on television and in fashion, the ones passed down in the bloodstream of our churches and families. They are the similarities I find whenever I look in the mirror, the characteristics I inherited from a baby boom generation coupled with now Post-Modernism that begs me to compromise the Gospel I know is worth dying for. It is that death alone, the chance encounter of seeing my Lord face-to-face, that I want to speak about in the next chapter. It is so interesting to me to see the hand of God work throughout my relatively short life, challenging me to put into practice the severe and heart-pounding lessons I have learned. Each trial, each trip, was the stepping-stone to grab hold of the strength to endure the next. Dare I say I see that each day is that for me as well? Each day is another chance encounter with the God of Creation, a chance to glimpse at the Holy in every circumstance, a chance to see my God so personally.

jump

as I write these words, I am twenty-two years old, a veteran of trials and heartache. Seeing my grandfather die before my very eyes, getting humiliated through a large intestine disease that left me grasping for air, almost dying of a liver disease and receiving a transplant, fighting against the bastion of hell in my mind as I sought to make sense of a terrible divorce, chronic rejection of my transplanted liver for almost five years, getting all six feet of my large intestine removed in one quick surgery, defecating in a bag for eight weeks and almost dying from extreme pain, wishing for death and praying for it every day, having the fear of the possibility of another liver transplant, taking large amounts of medication twice a day, drug induced diabetes, having a tube in my liver for over two years, and all the pain in between the lines, and now I was finally healed. But was I?

A week after I got back from China, a week after the most incredible trip of my life, and I was bedridden. While over there, I must have eaten something terrible, for I came back with an infection in the pouch section of my small intestine. Irritated to say the least, I lost almost thirty pounds from the amount of times I went to the bathroom, and my eyes started turning the familiar color of yellow again. It must have been from the sheer damage done to my weakened body, but my liver disease came back in full force. And so I started the terrible journey of pain once again.

Amidst circumstances beyond my control, I flew in and out of the hospital for the next few weeks or so and was able to get my liver functions back to normal. But I wasn't really scared during this time because I thought I was healed. Not having any direction besides my desire to finish school, I moved to a place that was familiar, a place that was comfortable, a place I called home. Mammoth was the next logical step in my life, and I moved up there with eager expectations to start a new life with all of the hope of no more pain and no more worry. I applied for a teaching job at my church up in Crowley Lake and received it with open arms and found myself starting lesson plans for the fall of 2000. I was going to be the next Crowley Lake Church on the Mountain junior high teacher. Telling them that there wouldn't be a need to worry or fear of another transplant in my near future, I promised to teach for at least a year.

My relationship with those kids grew by leaps and bounds, and I became more of an older brother than a teacher, waking up early in the morning consistently for the first time in my life and having a responsibility far greater than I at first perceived. I was their source of knowledge in all subjects and had to brush up on my skills like you wouldn't believe. My greatest fear was having to teach mathematics to a bunch of seventh-graders. I don't know why, but that part of the day was usually a time when the kids would open up to me about their problems with other kids, problems with their parents, and problems with life. I was their mentor; they were my little brothers and sisters, and we enjoyed a relationship that went far beyond any student/teacher relationship I had while growing up. I wanted to facilitate the best experience with those kids and tried doing the things that I always had wanted my teachers to do. One of my class's favorite times was when I cancelled half of their workload on Fridays and spent the latter half of the day watching a movie or hanging out and playing games. That time was known as Fiesta Fridays and came to be somewhat of a tradition.

Late into the first semester, in early November, something happened to me again that left me in a peculiar state. Since I was seen as these kids' ideal for a Christian brother and how they viewed a follower of Christ, I had to be the epitome of a Christian leader and warrior. When my eyes turned yellow and my energy level dissipated, they noticed. They noticed when I became irritable, they noticed when I was tired, and they noticed when I wasn't walking the way I taught. I have never felt more accountability towards my actions and the way I handled trials then during that time. Added to that, I had decided to show through example what it meant to put your trust in God, for it was then that I was dying.

Each day that I would come to class, with the color of my eyes in full glory, I would notice the concerned look on their faces and the way they began to treat me—no longer just as a brother in the sense that our culture understands it today, but more as a loved one who needed compassion and smiles. They grew up a little bit during that time, for they held the burden of death itself, as they beheld it with their eyes and felt it with my touch. But I grew up, too, and to this day, I am indebted to a bunch of kids who showed me what it meant to pick up my cross daily and apply the things that I had for so long studied in the Holy Scriptures. I wanted to show them what it meant to have Christ as the Rock, as the Cornerstone of our faith, and that putting our faith and trust in Him was not just something that happened when things were going smoothly but is the foundation to how we live our lives. It was at that point, in the middle of November, when the doctors told me that my liver was failing for the last time and could no longer function as it should.

All of the past five and a half years I had been struggling with rejection in such a way that it left me exhausted. In fact, I can remember earlier that summer, before my healing and before my trip to China, saying to myself and to God, "There is no way that I will go through another liver transplant. I will surely let my life go and die, for it is too terrible and too difficult. I no longer want to live this life as it is, just let me come home if it comes to that." Here I was, faced with the very real possibility of death again, knowing that a transplant, though long overdue, was the only option save eternity's blissful state with God in my final and very real home. What was I to do?

With the kids watching my every move, and with the Lord working miracles in my life in the form of strength and courage, I resolved to carry the banner of Christ one more time in the form of a transplant. In retrospect, to put it in visual terms I felt like Mel Gibson at the end of "The Patriot," when he picked up the flag of our nation and turned the battle's tide to ensure victory for those fighting for independence. It was my time, once again, to take all of my previous experiences, sift those through my mind, and move forward with what God was allowing me to go through. His banner was fixed in my mind and I decided to take it to my death, waving high the name of the Lord and the grace He had given me to live thus far.

It was then that I realized my life wasn't called to be normal, and at that time when I found out my call was different. Though it took me forever to realize this, I no longer wanted the life of everyone else. Content with what I was given, I didn't run from this transplant as I had so many times before. I finally was able to trust God in His perfect plan that absolutely—and don't get me wrong on this—made no sense to me nor anyone in contact with me. But there was still one thing lacking, actually there are still a thousand things lacking, but I hadn't fully surrendered my will and my plan for God's. Though His was perfect, and in my mind I believed in His sovereignty completely, my heart and soul still needed a little molding. Not until the hospital did this all come together. Not until my encounter with God Himself and His holiness did it ring true for me. In the world of my Platonic Dualism where matter and spirit are at complete odds—and sorry for throwing that term out at this stage in the book—I had always unknowingly separated my mind from my heart. I had always separated my knowledge of God from my entire body, never fully taking the step from knowledge of God to the application of His truth, namely, Christ dying for me. It was that truth acted out and actualized in my near death that formed me, completing me and enabling me to fully surrender not just my ideas and plans and knowledge, but my actual self as well.

It was December, and I had just enjoyed the last weekend I was going to have before the time I would be admitted to the hospital once again. Three of my closest friends at the time drove up from San Diego to Mammoth Lakes and spent an incredibly bonding and encouraging time with me. Jeff Block, Sam Kobielush, and Don Norton all drove up and spent my last hours before inevitable pain with me as we reminisced about the times we had shared together at Point Loma, at the View, and in the dorms at Young Hall. I was refreshed with life and was able to share with them my willingness and almost zeal for holding Christ's name high as I went through possible death once again. It was truly a blessing.

I was admitted to the hospital December 4, 2000, and I found that I was in an open room with many beds and a loud couple of roommates. When I say loud, I mean in respect to their bodily functions which we won't get in to, but needless to say, it was not the warmest welcome I have ever had. I knew I had stepped into reality when I was told that I had to put the hospital gown on and take off my regular clothes, something I wasn't too eager to do, and I felt the pull of memories surge through me like a tidal wave. People use the term "butterflies in their stomachs," but at that moment, it was more like rushing elephants playing soccer with a bowling ball. Suppressing the nerves was no easy task as I frequented the communal bathroom that stood in stark contrast to the comfort of my home. Now, later in life, it is no easy task to hold down the nauseous feelings whenever I get a whiff of something similar to the "clean" stench of the hospital.

That night, I wrote in my journal certain thoughts and worries I had, as a friend of mine mentioned the importance that this trial was going to play in the future of my life. I wanted to make sure I would remember everything. "Everything" in my mind included eager expectations of a quick transplant, not unlike that of my first. *Lord, let it be so.*

I can't remember what I was dreaming exactly, but I can tell you the very details of my sheets and the angle of the television when I was awoken. With sleep still in my eyes and a haze still in my mind, I looked over at the clock, and it read 6:30 a.m. My mother had not yet arrived, for she had decided to sleep at her friend's house where we used to live and commute to the hospital from there. Located about an hour away, it meant that she would usually arrive between 8:00 a.m. and 9:00 a.m. The reason why I remember everything in the room, though in my state of sleepiness, was because the nurse told me something that has changed me forever.

She woke me up asked if I needed anything (in order to stall for what she was going to tell me), and matter-of-factly said these words that I will never forget: "Mr. Parkins, I feel it necessary for you to know that you have less than twenty-four hours to live. Your INR count in your blood (that is, the blood coagulation ability) has elevated to over seven times the regular amount and you cannot move. If you have to go to the bathroom, buzz me in and I will give you a pan or a urinal. Your brain should be hemorrhaging and you should be bleeding profusely out of every joint. Once again, please do not attempt to move."

Now maybe it is just me, but I don't think you should *ever* tell someone that. It is argued that it is important to let someone know their particular state and where they stand, as far as health goes, but let them know *far* ahead of time, not *hours* before their projected death.

I was floored, and with those penetrating words that could not be worse, my heart sank. I remember her walking out of the room, probably to see another patient, and never seeing her again, though it was very odd that I didn't. Maybe she was called down from another floor to give me such news since it had to be incredibly difficult to do. Still, I was left there, some kid with a history of pain as far as he could remember, trying to breath for want of reality. *What was reality?*

Numb, I didn't call my mother for some reason but just sat there in bed, staring at the wall ahead of me, perplexed to say the least, ravished with confusion and immobility. They say your life "flashes" before your eyes right before you die. There was no "flash," only a slow, painful search of whether there had been anything that I had done for anyone besides myself. Shamefully, I bawled. My entire life,

I had faithfully gone to church, sometimes even six times a week. I knew more about the Bible than most people twice my age because of my studies, and though I never really was a "bad" person, I knew in my heart that I was incredibly selfish. I hadn't done anything with the "talents" God had given me; I hadn't done really anything with my faith.

After I had just sat there for about a half an hour or so, I looked at the clock and said to myself in utter disbelief, "Wow, I have less than twenty-three and a half hours to live." My time was ticking away, and I felt the pain of a disobedient child who said he cared for the things of his Creator, but never really did anything to prove it. I wasn't scared by any stretch of the imagination, which to this day leaves me content, but I was ashamed. It wasn't a matter of salvation, but I had been given the greatest gift called life, no matter how hard it had seemed, and I had done nothing with it. Sure, God may have used me numerous times to touch different people's lives, yet I had never really consciously done anything, or rather, intentionally done anything. I sat there and cried, not because I was going to die, for that truthfully was a welcomed thing, but because I had been so consumed with myself and my trials for my entire life, that I never really thought outside myself. I never lived for God, I just lived in God.

It was in that moment, and I stand by this as sure as I am sitting here typing this book, that God actually spoke to me. Now, I don't want to worry the reader, it wasn't some psychological phenomenon based on a rush of adrenaline or whatever that produced a ringing in my ear that I perceived to be the voice of God. No, it was actually His voice speaking to me, very personally and very plainly. It wasn't some theophany, nor was it like a burning bush that spoke to Moses. It wasn't some whisper that was barely audible, either. It sounded like a regular voice, only much fuller if that makes sense. It surrounded me, better than any surround sound theater and more personal than an angel's touch (not that I know, but it sounds good). It just seemed right and true, with words that still wake me up in the middle of the night from its memory or shake me up when I doubt.

I am sorry that I can't explain it better than that, but I don't need to. He said to me, "Dan, how much do you trust Me?"

Shock and doubt consumed me until I heard it again, "How much do you trust Me?"

What do you say to something like that? In truth, I answered with a whisper, for I was scared and amazed. "What do You mean, I thought I trusted You with everything. Look at my trials."

Again, the words, "How much do you trust Me?" surrounded me, encapsulating me to where I broke down and wept. I knew I couldn't trust my own plans, and I knew I couldn't trust the plans of the doctors,' for they pronounced my imminent death with little hope. Those thoughts raced through my head as I finally realized what He meant in that question. Was I finally now, after everything I had gone through, willing to give God my life and trust Him with it, or was I still going to rely on my own strength, wisdom, and being?

DREAMING INTO REALITY

The wind was howling at my back as I found myself atop a huge scraggly cliff that was so high and looming that I couldn't see the bottom below. Many things were racing through my mind, memories of ages past when I had been here before, and visions of what could be in the future, but the present was all that mattered. What was I doing there?

I could feel the hair on my skin stand on its own as the cold chill of the biting wind swept its way underneath my thin jacket that offered no protection. I wasn't wearing a hat, nor was I wearing a wool beanie that I almost coveted at that moment, but I had my dusty blonde hair open to the elements and the damaging effects of the torrent. In my hand I felt a large wooden pole, very slick and finished, with a hardness I had felt before. It seemed to be an extension of me, though for the life of me I couldn't recount of the tales when I had carried it before. It didn't matter, I was there now, and I was holding a long wooden pole in my hand that seemed to be a banner of some sort.

Cackling could be heard behind me as I almost turned around to face it. I can't explain it, but turning around would have been the death of me, and I knew it, for I would surely have lost my footing and would have fallen to my death in the chasm below. What was that man laughing at? The cackling and cajoling grew louder and louder as the wind grew more fierce, almost pushing me over the cliff in its own right. The banner caught the wind as a sail and almost flung me over the cliff, also, and I quickly realized that I was in a very precarious situation. What was I to do? Turning around would be an admittance that I couldn't handle where I was, yet was that a bad thing? Everyone else would have turned around, and I knew it; so somehow, through the strength that had been borne in me, I stayed there and prayed, hoping that God would give me some sort of justice or honor in not turning.

Ground gave way beneath my feet as I stepped backwards to avoid the fall, barely making it to steady my balance lest I fall. What the heck does all this mean? Why do I feel like I can't turn around, Lord? The laughing grew almost unbearable as I could feel the hot breath of the enemy behind my back, fingers and hands inches away from pushing me down that chasm.

A thought came to me, and I shoved the banner pole firmly in the ground screaming, "No! I will not die here!" With that steadiness came a certainty that I wasn't going to die easily, and I gritted my teeth in determination. The banner itself made its familiar noises as it flapped with and against the wind, shining in its own glory. I looked at what the banner said, what I was carrying, and closed my eyes. Lord, what do I do? I have been here for so long, so long that I can't remember a time when I wasn't at this cliff. Take me away, make me somewhere else.

Tears were streaming down my cheeks as they etched out rivers of skin through my face. I was a mess, and I needed to find rest in His arms. I wanted so badly to turn around and find more familiar ground, ground not so perilous as this. My knees started shaking from sheer exhaustion, almost failing and then regaining some semblance of balance. Can't I just turn around quickly to survey what was behind me? My Lord, what should I do?

A thunderous voice boomed, "Jump."

"Jump?!" I asked incredulously, "Are you kidding me?" That's exactly what the enemy wants. "He wants me to die!"

"Jump."

God, that can't be you? Why on earth do You want me to jump? That makes absolutely no sense and . . . no, I can't do it. I have been here so long carrying Your banner amidst the battle that has been ongoing around me, and now You are asking me to give all of that up, as if it didn't really matter?

The breath of the enemy was on me and the screaming cackle shook my eardrums to their core. Losing hearing almost instantaneously, I felt the trickle of blood flow out of my ears down my neck. I was getting worse. The laughter stopped and beckoned me, "Dan, all you have to do is turn around. It isn't that big of a deal. You can do it. Just turn around for crying out loud! You want to stay on this cliff forever? I didn't think so, just turn around and everything will be okay."

Crying my last tear, I heard that boom again, "Jump."

"But I will die. I don't want to die, Lord, I don't want to die."

"How much do you trust Me? Jump."

And with those final words, I had no choice. To turn around would surely kill me, so I did as the Lord told me. Bending down, I heard through my deafness a screaming hysteria, imagining wild eyes in terror as I gathered all of the strength left in me and jumped off of the cliff. Victory, finally.

With that action done, and the wind whisking away the hair from my face as I flew through the air, I realized in complete satisfaction that I wasn't falling. My body felt free for the first time in my life, with all of the aches and pains gone. I didn't even have to go to the bathroom, and the pains in my stomach had virtually disappeared. What was so amazing was what I felt on my back. Unknown to me, God had given me wings, and I was soaring, finally with Him, finally able to give Him everything that I was. And in the distance I heard a voice not so loud as a boom, spoken by one of God's prophets saying, "Even youths grow tired and weary, and young men stumble and fall; but those who hope in the Lord will renew their strength. They will soar on wings like eagles; they will run and not grow weary, they will walk and not be faint." It was time for me to fly.

I never had to have another daydream again.

AWAKENING

I was at a crossroads, for all of my life I had ridden on the backs of the other trials, getting my strength from the knowledge and experience of them. I felt that I was strong enough to get through each one, believing what people had said about me. But God, in effect, was saying that though the trials were significant, they can't carry me past the next one. Though they were important in my sanctification process that is still going on to this day, I couldn't rely on them. Each new trial, and each new day for that matter, we come to this crossroads. Are we going to trust Him today with whatever we are going to deal with, or are we going to try to do it on our own? I believe He asks us all that in every single one of our trials, as well as temptations. But this encounter with God, this actual encounter, left me speechless. Finally now, after all I had been through, I saw the truth of God. I saw that He asks us to be like those little children who run to their daddy's arms, or the ones who jump off the edge of the pool into his grasp. Do I trust Him with just this part of my life, or do I trust Him with everything? Do I trust Him only in my trials, or do I trust Him with finances and everything else? How much do I really trust God? How much am I willing to forgo everything that society is emphatically shoving down my throat, needless to say what the doctors themselves said, and trust God?

The sad thing is most people think this is too simple. That this doesn't give them enough explanation nor reason to release is reason enough to take the steering wheel once again and assume control. Yeah, like we have *any* control to begin with?

When I heard those words, I was finally able to transfer my knowledge to my heart and give up the battle I had long been losing with God. Now I don't want to suggest that the trials were the battlefield to that war, but I do know that I didn't die that day. I put my trust in Him completely and closed my eyes and ran to my Savior who accepts me for who I am. And as the daydream says in the final paragraph, I soared that day on "wings like eagles." But that was just the second day I was in the hospital. It turns out that I was in that place for more than two months, fighting harder, learning more, and getting more encouragement from the Lord than I ever have. It was truly amazing, and I wouldn't take it back for all the tea in China.

interpretation

i don't remember the first couple of days I was in the Intensive Care Unit at UCLA Hospital, but I can remember waking up on the third or fourth day one morning, thankful to be alive. I was so revitalized from my latest brush with death that it gave me the energy and comfort to get through what followed. And what followed—in what I liken to be the closest to hell I have ever experienced—was an incredibly wonderful, yet trying time; wonderful in the sense of actual wonder at God's comfort and personal touch in my life, and trying in the sense that I was faced with many more trials. I wrote this in my journal:

Second Thursday Night:

I am so blessed, Lord; all power and glory are Yours forever. Saying that last sentence seems so right for some reason. I wish my limited vocabulary could express more clearly Your unlimited characteristic of love. You are holy and just, and in Your name alone I find comfort, let alone Your loving arms. At night, when my thoughts drift to You, I am refreshed and cooled by Your wonderful promises. Lord Jesus, I trust You completely, so I ask in Your name that You wrap those caressing arms and embrace my frail body . . . I ask Lord, by Your power, that the enemy will have no victory in or by my body, forever more . . . Even now, war is waged in my naked body, and I fight the attacks on my own ground. Upon going to the bathroom, nothing but blood is released from my bowels. This first happened yesterday, and You gave me the wisdom to smile at Satan's feeble attempts to penetrate Your servant's temple, housing Your Holy Spirit. I trust You Lord, so I am not afraid, but I ask that You bind any more attacks from this needle-pierced body. Thank You, Lord, for Your strength. You will bring it to pass.

I was dealing with something very painful as I was feeling the effects of a disease head on. This journal entry, written on the third Saturday night I was in ICU, explains plainly and simply what I was dealing with:

Almost twenty-one days now, and my position on this bed has changed very little, though my weakened body has changed much. You have given me grace to smile, though inwardly I have grown to remember what aching pain feels like from the growth of my liver and pancreas suffocating my small intestine. Diseased fatty tissue is growing around my failing liver, and my confused pancreas is struggling with the notion of trying to do the liver's job as well. Consequently, after every meal that I consume, the food tries to pass through constricted portions of my intestine, providing for me a strong painful sensation that I heartily do not recommend. Though I write about it blandly, I want You to realize that I am exhausted. I feel as if my cookie jar of strength that You have given me grace to take hold of is almost diminished, though I must remember that I am Your child and I refuse to worry.

Each morning I would wake up, and the nurses would attempt to draw blood from the IVs that had found a home in my veins, as those IVs seemed to beckon the veins to collapse so they could find a new host to destroy. It was always frightening when at first they would not be able to draw any more blood, and that always made me leery to wake up each morning. I had tubes connected to two IVs, electric monitors hooked up to six places on my chest and stomach, and to top it all off, I had to wear the "oh so fashionable" hospital garb. Almost four weeks were spent that way, and each time I had to go to the bathroom, as you can guess by now through my story that it was quite often, I had to ask permission and went in a small bowl next to my bed.

One of the scariest times that I experienced while in the ICU was when I first stood up from that little bowl, in my weakened condition and found before me a horror. If you can imagine squatting over a plastic bowl, nothing to rest on save the strength of your weakened legs, and lifting up after a brief time to find chunks of dark blood, similar to muddy red Jell-O, lining the container. Graphic, yes, but as much as reading this made you queasy, they were *my* eyes that witnessed it first hand, coming out of *my* body. But, at this time in my life, I shrugged it off and "laughed" that Satan would try to get at me that way once again. As mentioned earlier in my first journal entry, it was very difficult to deal with but something I had grown accustomed, and the strength God had given me was enough to get through any boulder rolled my way.

But the time did indeed wear on me in the Intensive Care Unit, and I found myself weakened at points. Each day was like a nightmare as far as experiences go, for I had never witnessed death as I had that month. Not the aspect of death for me, but I heard death at least twice a night, sometimes more. I wrote about it on the second Saturday night, the 17th of December:

The time is late right now, passing twelve midnight with one swift stroke, and insomnia is slowly becoming more and more of a reality for me. I have again learned a valuable lesson tonight, for I smile no more in the face of Satan. Truth be known, I grit my teeth in determination when he wounds me with sounds of death. Directly to the left of my intensive care station I hear a woman fighting insanity in her head as she struggles with two people inside her, one moment a sweet old lady, the next using language to make the most strong of heart very feeble. I truly feel like she is possessed by powers not of this world. My attention is drawn to the station beyond hers from the sound of a medical doctor yelling, "Clear!" Although repeated attempts are made, they cannot hold off the inevitable, and the computer rings with a flat monotone voice. Across the way I hear sobs as a large family is forced to pull the plug and take their grandfather off the respiratory system. All of this is shadowed by the prayers and chimes of an unknown Arabian family pleading to an unknown God for the sake of saving an unknown person. So now, Lord, I tell You that I have no smiles directed at Satan, only towards Your loving arms. Open them wide for me because I am running to You. Give me a double portion of Your strength and allow me to bask in Your warmth and light. I want to be blinded by You until all that I am is consumed. I trust You that you are teaching me something . . . let me forgive and forget each morning of the battles I have to go through, and refresh my body with the little sleep I receive.

On the 28th of December, I received my second liver transplant and had to struggle with the dichotomy of life—that my life was enabled to go on through the death of another. The man I received the liver from was one who died in a rock climbing accident and was the same age as me. That was all I was allowed to know about him, for contact with his family was only allowed through a letter that my mother wrote. It was very hard for her to write a second letter, but she was able to share our hope through their loss, which couldn't have done much as far as comfort for that family. God is in control and I have to believe that only His plan is perfect, not mine or anyone else's.

Complications soon arose from the transplant, for my immune system was non-existent, and my body had been in a weakened state due to the liver disease and the long time in the hospital. We all carry with us a virus known as Ecoli, one that enables the average person to digest their food properly and more efficiently. However, in my sorry state, my body was not even able to fight off this seemingly benign creature, and it attacked my pancreas with reckless abandon. Abscesses formed around one of the only organs in my body that I could count on to function normally, and the pain quickly grew insurmountable. The pain reminded me quickly of that wicked time in Mammoth when I had that abdominal pain from the possible gangrene; I grew hard and confused.

Seven days later, with the pain coming in slower spurts, the doctors released me, not knowing I still had problems that needed immediate attention. They had no clue that the virus was attacking my pancreas and agreed amongst themselves that I was just having problems passing my stools and that the pain would go away in a short time. I, however, did not share their optimism, but I welcomed my release from the hospital, I welcomed a shower, and I welcomed a soundless room consisting of my mother in a bed beside mine, just a few feet away.

That first night in my newly converted hospital room, which was an actual hotel room less than a mile away from the hospital, proved to be one of drowning pain and intense conflict in my mind. In the early stages of my medication, I received strong dosages which toyed with my thoughts and manipulated my thinking. That is all I can say to describe it, for I was not myself and wanted to give up on the situation. My stomach was full of staples, with dried blood not yet scabbed over, and completely bloated like a pregnant woman's belly. *How horrible was that?* I remember taking a shower that first night, gingerly stepping beneath the showerhead, sitting on a waterproof white chair that held the weight my legs couldn't. Feeling the water pound my head, cleansing my thinking, reminding me of trust, and renewing my energy, I resolved to get through this no matter what. I had to.

And that first night was terrible. Sleep was only a dream I wished I had, and I spent the night pressing on my stomach with a white pillow as to apply pressure. The doctors had told me that because of the increased bloating, my staples were stretching and ripping, bringing on more pain with each breath and with each bite of food I ate. The pillow was meant to counteract what the bloating was doing, but much to my chagrin, it acted more as a catalyst to the pain than anything else.

Not an ounce of sleep found me that night, as I was constantly moaning and trying fervently to suppress my urge to scream and holler. *Lord, why are you still allowing this to happen? I told You I trust You, now take this away and get me out of here! How long must I continue to go through this? Please Lord, I have learned enough for now, release me from the bondage of pain I feel every second.*

Morning came rather slowly, crawling and inching its way to our window that overlooked a series of buildings. Like a wounded soldier dragging its near lifeless body over our newly vacuumed carpet, the sunshine made its way to reveal six o'clock in the morning. My mother, having only a few hours of sleep herself, found me bundled in the bloated ball position and began to cry some more. Within a couple of hours, I was back in the hospital bed, eagerly awaiting my first shot of morphine to take away the pain.

They reopened my wound in my stomach to do "exploratory surgery" and found the abscesses tucked away around my poor pancreas. A month later, amidst struggles for sanity and strength, I emerged from the hospital a changed and weathered man, a seasoned soldier with the scars to prove it. Naïveté somewhat lost, beaten, broken and without pride, I came February 4, 2001 to Mammoth Lakes, beautiful Mammoth Lakes.

The war was over, for the most part. I had been beaten, but my army had victory. I was wounded, but I would heal. I had fallen, but God graced me with the strength to raise my face from the mud, look around, and slowly get up. I should be dead, but I was alive. Knowing that was somehow enough, somehow reason to say "No" to the lies that spoke otherwise. I was breathing, I was sleeping, and I was eating in my own bed . . . the bed that always found me and refreshed me.

TRUSTING

I was indeed able to travel and speak for a couple of months after I had strength to walk, but quickly became weak from the constant driving and travel, so I resolved to help start a church group for college-aged kids in San Diego, California. After that had gotten underway, I found myself starting another college group out in Palm Desert, California, called Siren Project. As I near the end of writing my story, I am twenty-seven years old, married, and working to further the Kingdom of God. Do I still travel and speak? Yes, but my passion is for the college students in the Escondido Valley of San

Diego; that is where I am hoping to make an impact. I take over forty pills a day, still after over two years am insulin dependent as a drug-induced diabetic, and constantly go to the bathroom more than most.

As I read my story I still get tears at how good God is . . . all the time. I am alive, and that is more than I deserve. So what if I still deal with pain every day? So what that my life might be harder than most? I am alive, and each day, I have committed to serving the Lord in any capacity I am able to. He has given me this day to serve Him, and that, I can say with confidence, is the reason we are all still breathing.

In the end, after all is said and done, now that I am able to look back on all of my trials, I realize that each one was a gift. Yet, during the midst of the tempest, if anyone tried to convince me that those storms were mere "gifts," I would go into a rage as the definitions of those storms suggest.

Jesus was radical, and, in his radical ministry, moved us to think differently about the world we dwell. His entire Sermon on the Mount suggests the unwavering notion of being "set apart," completely contradictory to the world and its standards. Yet, so many of us try to mix the standards of this world—what it holds as absolute truth, which is really no truth at all—with God's perfect standard, the Word. Why is this so? In viewing things such as love, are we conditional? Absolutely. How about forgiveness and tolerance? Again, those standards of excellence that God puts forth are intermingled with lies full of empty promises and slogans. Are we not supposed to view *everything* differently than what the world has defined? Yes! That is the most important issue that I am trying to face. As in daydreams, we are all not ourselves, wistfully wishing away pain and heartache. It is time to wake up and no longer live within the confines of our supposed imaginations. What I mean is we are indeed different, as Christians, and everything we view, now with eyes hopefully unclouded through the assertions in the Word of God, should be measured with that truth.

Look at how we currently view trials. We see them as the ultimate evil, and at times they may seem that way, and feel completely valid in that way of thinking, yet if we are truly radical in our thinking, we will begin to see them as gifts. What else do we need to view radically? I say everything, for anything mixed with the seemingly absurd claims of the Bible turns out to be nothing more than convenience. An example of this can be seen in dating relationships and how even Christian couples have tried to compromise.

A friend of mine just began a relationship with a girl from the college group I now oversee. He told me himself that he didn't think that he was ready but greatly desired the companionship that this new relationship was going to offer. Does he have the knowledge to be able to lift her up, growing her closer to the Lord in everything they do? Absolutely not, yet in his mind, he sees that it is okay. "Dan, we aren't doing anything bad, I haven't even kissed her, yet."

What he doesn't realize is that he is quickly going down the road the enemy so desperately desires him to go, compromise. Compromise with the standards of society so that he can in "good conscience" date a woman he has no business dating. All of his friends tell him that it is good, even his parents affirming this, yet he isn't even spiritually fit to lead himself. Why does he think that he can do any good for this girl, hoping to show her Christ through his actions, when he doesn't even know Christ's words to be relevant enough to follow closely? But such is the train of thought, such is the philosophy of blood that coerces through our veins. If Christ calls us to be radically different than the world, and indeed we know this, why do we fight it so much, that we can make little compromises to have what our flesh cries out for? He wants the relationship, yet he doesn't want the God-given relationship God has in store for him. This is the sad state of affairs we find ourselves. Is it any wonder why we can't get free from the world?

We can't get free no matter how hard we try, for we are constantly trying to mix two standards that are completely at war with each other. Take Christian living, for example. I have a friend who lives in Irvine, California in a very upscale neighborhood, who is faced with the "dilemma" of marrying a pastor. She is so afraid to marry him because she isn't sure she will be able to afford the trips to Hawaii or the perfect cars she has planned out in her mind. And where did she get those standards? Surely not from the Bible, yet she holds to them as if they were her God-given right. Where do we get such absurd claims? "But I want them," she proclaims, "I should at least be able to have those things." As if the cars and trips to Hawaii were somehow between the lines of "blessed are the poor in spirit."

We view trials the same way. "I don't deserve this trial, I deserve this kind of life . . ." There is no theology to back this up, no scriptural references when taken in context. My God does not promise an easy life, or He would already be a liar. But he promises to be there. There is a lie that says with our faith we will be prosperous in the world, such a reference in the Bible does not exist, only in the perplexities and enigmas that are hidden in television, books, movies, and sometimes, spoken forth from pulpits. Society says that trials are terrible, but if we truly looked at them in light of what scripture says, we would get an entirely different story. Trials mold us, they shape us into what Christ calls us to be—set apart. That is why sanctification is such an intimate process, and that is why trials rip us to our cores. They are stark reminders, with Christ as our presupposition, that we are different, and we need to view them differently.

Still not convinced? Christ calls us to pick up our crosses daily, our instruments of death and carry them around with us. Society calls us to make life as easy as possible, avoiding things that are difficult. Christ calls us to be poor in spirit, yet the world says to be rich and prideful in spirit, not letting anyone get the best of you. He pleads with us through His apostle Paul to rather be wronged than to take a brother to court, yet how many Christians do you see waging war in those wooden coffins of debate? I could write an entire book devoted to the subject of how we are admonished to be, think, and act differently than the world we reside in. Should it be any wonder that our views of trials need to be looked at in such a way as well?

Yet trials are personal. Trials are painful to our cores. They rip us open and leave us gasping for anything to stop the flow of blood that drains us of life. They are the archenemy, terrible to behold and awful

daydreams // an end to my nightmares

to go through. We say, "No one knows what I am going through," though we expect sympathy and a certain measure of empathy every time. Most of the time, trials make us focus on only two things: ourselves and then God.

The first thing we tend do is think about ourselves whenever faced with a crossroads or pain in life. "Why is this happening to *me*?" Then the emphasis of the question gets put on something else. "*Why is* this happening to me," beckoning our Creator to answer. Most of us, however, never get past that discouraging first step. We stop and dwell on ourselves. Constantly, all we can think about is our current state, how nothing else in our past has ever been this hard, and how no one understands. This is the antithesis of truth, yet most of us reside in this thinking like mildew in a bathtub.

It is imperative to now turn the focus off of ourselves and onto the God who exudes sovereignty with every decision. God, the God who allows certain pain in our lives, certain heartache and confusion for His glory—and remember, we live for God's glory and not our own—ordained before the creation of the world the suffering, trials, and pain of His own Son for an incredible purpose . . . our redemption and the redemption of the Church. Acts 2.23 and 4.27–28 give evidence of this:

> "This man, delivered over by the predetermined plan and foreknowl-
> edge of God, you nailed to a cross by the hands of godless men and
> put Him to death . . . For truly in this city there were gathered together
> against your holy servant Jesus, whom you anointed, both Herod and
> Pontius Pilate, along with the Gentiles and the peoples of Israel, to do
> whatever your hand and your purpose predestined to occur."

It was God's decision and control, His utter and complete sovereign design that allowed His Son to be crucified for our sakes. Do you think that God wanted that to happen, that He took joy in that decision? If there was joy, it was because of what that act accomplished, the absolute removal of any sin once the gift of faith is administered to our hearts. I don't think God was up in heaven, rubbing His hands together like a sadistic mad man, dwelling on the sufferings of His own Son, yet He allowed it to happen because of the infinite goodness that would occur. I also do not and cannot believe in a God who was not powerful enough to stop such a horrendous act. Post Modern thought has so crept into some of our seminaries and theological thinking that it has deceived some into thinking that God is not completely sovereign. But He is, and when we look at our trials in light of this, we become desperate to understand God's great design. This is completely understandable, for even the disciples were completely confused and stayed in a state of shock before they had the risen Christ actualized in their midst.

The afflictions of Jesus were not only predestined to occur, but also necessary beyond any doubt. If Christ's afflictions and trials were for our own good, it would follow that our trials are for our own good as well. Philippians 1.29 says, "*For to you it has been granted for Christ's sake, not only to believe in Him, but also to suffer for His sake.*" Romans 5.3–5, "*Not only so, but we also rejoice in our sufferings, because we know that suffering produces perseverance; perseverance, character; and character, hope. And hope does not disappoint us, because God has poured out His love into our hearts by the Holy Spirit, whom He has given us.*"

Second Corinthians, Chapter One speaks plainly about why it is that we go through trials, though it may not be something you want to hear and it may bring absolutely no comfort to the reader. To me, however, it makes perfect sense. Listen to Paul and where he has landed in his journey to understand the pain and suffering in his life. Verse 7–9 say:

> "And our hope for you is firm, because we know that just as you share in our sufferings, so also you share in our comfort. We do not want you to be uninformed, brothers, about the hardships we suffered in the province of Asia (Minor). We were under great pressure, far beyond our ability to endure, so that we despaired even of life. Indeed, in our hearts we felt the sentence of death. But this happened that we might not rely on ourselves but on God, who raises the dead."

Throughout all of my pain, throughout all of my trials, I realized that I wasn't allowed to go through them so that I may know how strong (weak) I actually was, so that I could rely on myself, but so that I might realize the goodness and strength of God and rely and rest on Him. Did I have the strength to deal with two liver transplants? Did I have the strength to deal with betrayal and an emotional rift even in the midst of those transplants? Was there no reason for those trials, only happening to me because God was not powerful to stop them? Did they happen to me because God can be compared to a sad, angry, mad man, sadistic in His very being? Is there no God and these things happened to me in whimsical fashion? Or was there an intimate God behind those trials, allowing them to transpire for my own eternal benefit?

If sanctification is the process of becoming more holy, more like the Son of God I love with a passion, then does it not make comforting sense that God allows this pain in our lives that we might learn God's lordship through each passing trial? Christ realized in His life that He could do nothing without the Father, and if we are to be more like Christ, don't these heartaches show us little by little to rely not on ourselves, but on the God whom Christ so desperately relied on as well? It is God's loving-kindness, His personal intimacy and touch, that brings us to our knees and brings our wills in conformity with His.

TRUTH

Break us Lord, show us how intimate You are with us through our trials, show us Your love and the beauty of Your holiness. Let us cry with David in Psalm 139 of Your comforting intimacy and Your personal touch.

> "O Lord, You have searched me and You know me. You know when I sit and when I rise; You perceive my thoughts from afar. You discern my going out and my lying down; You are familiar with all my ways. Before a word is on my tongue You know it completely, O Lord. You hem me in—behind and before; You have laid Your hand upon me, such knowledge is too wonderful for me, too lofty for me to attain. Where can I go from Your Spirit? Where can I flee from Your presence? If I go up to the

heavens, You are there; if I make my bed in the depths, You are there. If I rise on wings of the dawn, if I settle on the far side of the sea, even there Your hand will guide me, Your right hand will hold me fast . . . For You created my inmost being; You knit me together in my mother's womb. I praise You because I am fearfully and wonderfully made; Your works are wonderful, I know that full well . . . All the days ordained for me were written in Your book before one of them came to be. How precious to me are Your thoughts, O God! How vast is the sum of them! Were I to count them, they would outnumber the grains of sand . . . Search me, O God, and know my heart; test me and know my anxious thoughts. See if there is any offensive way in me, and lead me in the way everlasting."

Hebrews 12.6, "because the Lord disciplines those He loves and He punishes everyone He accepts as a son."

Job 1.21b, "The Lord gave and the Lord has taken away; may the name of the Lord be praised."

a goodbye

Pain and trials are never desired, yet history, even in our own lives, shows us the beauty of them. No amount of words could give comfort nor answer the question of "why" when someone experiences the death of a child or something similarly dreadful. No themes of God's sovereignty or of God's goodness to us would or could do justice in comforting us, though in fact may bring about rage and bitterness, yet we are faced with those who have had an encounter with God and see the questions strikingly disappear.

If pain would be a virus, it would be without a doubt the flu, the sickness that has killed more than any other, and one that, no matter how hard we try, we cannot find a cure. Why can we not find a cure? Influenza changes form, with variations numbering into the thousands, if not more, and we must get "flu shots" every new season because of this. It is no respecter of persons, regardless of race, creed, or preference, and it attacks all with little to no order. Though each person inevitably gets the flu, with rare exceptions, our bodies develop immunities in the form of antibodies to fight them. Yet, why does the flu come back year after year? Because it is stronger each time. We have the resistance to fight off the old one, but we need new shots and new antibodies to fight off the new strain.

Pain in our lives is frighteningly similar to the flu, yet exponentially more difficult to bear. Like the flu, trials plague every person with no exceptions: "righteous" or "unrighteous," good or bad, Christian or non-Christian. Our antibodies in pain are the familiarity of those trials, riding on the strength of the past to give us strength in the future or strength in the present circumstance. Each time that we get through a certain trial, we build up those antibodies through specific encounters with God. The platform for those encounters could be nature, friends, scripture, or a specific theophany of God. But if you search back, you can find encounters that pushed you forward amidst those trials. Like the flu, pain comes back to us in different ways, attacking us and invading our very core. As our immune system battles a war that is unseen in our bodies, so we wage war in our minds for comfort, control, understanding, and meaning amidst new and threatening trials. Old trials will give us only so much strength, but to conquer each new trial, we need fresh new encounters with the living God who gave us life in the first place.

I pray that, as you read my story, I showed you a glimpse of my encounters with God, my questions and my honesty. I desire for you to be refreshed through my testimony of God's handprint in my life (albeit a heavy one at times) coupled with the truth that I have gained. I don't presume that any of this will provide too much comfort, for that can only come through the working of the Holy Spirit. We are all traveling the road together, but my hope is that you will learn to recognize your own encounters through the telling of mine.

This relationship we have with Christ, who bids us to take up our crosses daily, to come and die, is not some meander, stroll or walk. It is a battle, and it is a run . . . often times straight up a rock face, but it is a race that we must run nonetheless. Though the experience of trials helps us, they cannot take us through the next leg of the journey alone. Those antibodies cannot fight off the onslaught of new pain, but the encounters with God, those times when He carries us when we are too weak to even breathe on the run, the "flu shot" that sends pearls of wisdom, are what takes us to the finish line. The realization that Christ is worth dying for is the presupposition we take with us and use as the means to which we filter our worldview. It is that worldview that helps us answer the question of why and with that paradigm shift that we erase the pressure of even asking why.

Throughout this book, I have made mention that we need to wake up from the "dreams" we are currently living out in our lives. We are content with living in the clouds of our misconceptions. But living in our daydreams of naïveté, having desire for control and the like, is allowing the enemy of all to rob us of the joy, not necessarily the happiness, that comes with trusting in a sovereign Lord who has a perfect plan for us all. Look at my life, please. I am no better than anyone, and no stronger than the mouse that invades my cupboards, for I possess no strength on my own accord. It is Christ who gave me the strength, and nothing else that allows me to have the testimony of pain, yet the life of love that I desire so strongly to live out. I have no bitterness, no feeling of being wronged. Quite the opposite in fact. Most of the time, the people with the most bitterness never trusted in God to begin with, and only used their own feeble strength to "get through" seemingly "impossible" trials. Our culture has deceived us into thinking that we are strong individuals and that we should rely on our own strength and wisdom. We see ourselves as the "masters" of our own destinies or "lords" of our lives. But God is my King, and it is in Him and His holiness and wisdom that I place my life willingly and irresistibly.

I pray that we all can wake up, violently if needed, and stop trying to "judge" the living God by what we as His creation see amidst the trials and pain, hurt and loss. The answers to all your questions will come, as they have for me, but in all, faith must reside. Faith, and a childlike trust. Proverbs 3.5–6 says, "*Trust in the Lord with all your heart, and lean not on your own understanding. In all your ways acknowledge Him, and He will make your paths straight.*"

I end with a hymn written by a man who himself knew immense trial and pain, William Cowper. The Hymn is called "God Moves in a Mysterious Way,"

> Judge not the Lord by feeble sense,
> But trust Him for His grace;
> Behind a frowning providence
> He hides a smiling face.
> His purposes will ripen fast,
> Unfolding every hour;
> The bud may have a bitter taste,
> But sweet will be the flower.

I pray that the Lord will bless you in your trials, as He has so abundantly blessed me in mine.

CONTACT

Daniel Parkins
639 E. 17th Street
Escondido, CA 92025
760.781.2221
dparkins@efcc.org
www.theremnanttour.com
http://www.myspace.com/sushi_pastor
http://www.myspace.com/theremnanttour

daydreams // an end to my nightmares

TATE PUBLISHING *& Enterprises*

Tate Publishing is commited to excellence in the publishing industry. Our staff of highly trained professionals, including editors, graphic designers, and marketing personnel, work together to produce the very finest books available. The company reflects the philosophy established by the founders, based on Psalms 68:11,

"THE LORD GAVE THE WORD AND GREAT WAS THE COMPANY OF THOSE WHO PUBLISHED IT."

If you would like further information, please call 1.888.361.9473 or visit our website www.tatepublishing.com

TATE PUBLISHING *& Enterprises*, LLC 127 E. Trade Center Terrace Mustang, Oklahoma 73064 USA